Comments on other *Amazing Stories* from readers & reviewers

"Tightly written volumes filled with lots of wit and humour about famous and infamous Canadians."
Eric Shackleton, *The Globe and Mail*

"The heightened sense of drama and intrigue, combined with a good dose of human interest is what sets Amazing Stories *apart."*
Pamela Klaffke, *Calgary Herald*

"This is popular history as it should be...For this price, buy two and give one to a friend."
Terry Cook, a reader from Ottawa, on **Rebel Women**

"Glasner creates the moment of the explosion itself in graphic detail...she builds detail upon gruesome detail to create a convincingly authentic picture."
Peggy McKinnon, *The Sunday Herald,* on **The Halifax Explosion**

"It was wonderful...I found I could not put it down. I was sorry when it was completed."
Dorothy F. from Manitoba on **Marie-Anne Lagimodière**

"Stories are rich in description, and bristle with a clever, stylish realness."
Mark Weber, *Central Alberta Advisor,* on **Ghost Town Stories II**

"A compelling read. Bertin...has selected only the most intriguing tales, which she narrates with a wealth of detail."
Joyce Glasner, *New Brunswick Reader,* on **Strange Events**

"The resulting book is one readers will want to share with all the women in their lives."
Lynn Martel, *Rocky Mountain Outlook,* on **Women Explorers**

AMAZING STORIES®

ISAAC BROCK

Canada's Hero in the War of 1812

Cheryl MacDonald

HISTORY

James Lorimer & Company Ltd., Publishers
Toronto

James Lorimer & Company Ltd., Publishers acknowledges the support of the Ontario Arts Council. We acknowledge the financial support of the Government of Canada through the Canada Book Fund for our publishing activities. We acknowledge the support of the Canada Council for the Arts which last year invested $24.3 million in writing and publishing throughout Canada. We acknowledge the Government of Ontario through the Ontario Media Development Corporation's Ontario Book Initiative.

  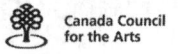

ONTARIO ARTS COUNCIL
CONSEIL DES ARTS DE L'ONTARIO

Canada Council
for the Arts

Cover image: © 2012 The States of Guernsey (Guernsey Museums & Galleries)

Library and Archives Canada Cataloguing in Publication

MacDonald, Cheryl, 1952-
Isaac Brock : Canada's hero in the War of 1812 / Cheryl MacDonald.

(Amazing stories)
Includes bibliographical references and index.
Issued also in electronic formats.
ISBN 978-1-4594-0059-7

1. Brock, Isaac, Sir, 1769-1812. 2. Generals--Canada--Biography. 3. Canada--History--War of 1812. I. Title. II. Series: Amazing stories (Toronto, Ont.)

FC443.B76M33   2012 971.03'2092   C2012-901948-8

James Lorimer & Company Ltd., Publishers
317 Adelaide Street West, Suite 1002
Toronto, ON, Canada
M5V 1P9
www.lorimer.ca

Printed and bound in Canada

For Roy Winders, who knows what it takes to lead men.

Contents

Prologue

October 13, 1812

Isaac Brock slept fitfully in his bed at Fort George. It was only a matter of time before the Americans attacked. Just a few hours earlier, Brigade-Major Thomas Evans had crossed the Niagara River from Queenston under a flag of truce and come back with disturbing news. The Americans were gathering boats, preparing to cross the river into Upper Canada.

Not completely convinced, Brock chose to stay at Fort George, 11 km upstream from Queenston. But he was worried, fully aware that his defences might crumble before an American onslaught. There were too few regular soldiers. Too few militia had seen combat, and Brock was still unsure of their loyalty. As for the natives—the victory at Detroit two months earlier had persuaded them that the British could keep the Americans at bay. But could they be trusted if the tide of battle turned in favour of the invaders?

Uncomfortable in his breeches, shirt, and stockings, Brock dozed. It was still dark when he was wakened by a messenger. The attack had begun! Leaping from his bed and barking orders, Brock pulled on his boots, was helped into his tunic, buckled on his sabre, and raced towards his horse.

Chapter 1
Early Years

The battle was raging at Egmont-op-Zee in the Netherlands, the air filled with smoke from the guns, the acrid odour of gunpowder, and the tang of salt. British and Russian forces, including the Forty-Ninth Regiment of Foot, were engaged in a battle with the French, pushing inland from the shore of the North Sea towards the town of Alkmaar.

Among the members of the Forty-Ninth were Savery Brock, not quite twenty-seven, paymaster and aide-de-camp to Lieutenant-General Sir Ralph Abercromby; and Sergeant James FitzGibbon, an eighteen-year-old Irish farm boy turned soldier who had never before been in battle. FitzGibbon watched in amazement mixed with fear as Savery raced from the top of one sand dune to another, rallying the soldiers, urging them to drive back the enemy. A tall, big-boned man,

Savery was an easy target for the opposing forces; FitzGibbon was convinced he would be shot down at any moment. But FitzGibbon was also impressed by Savery's courage and the way he inspired the troops, and made up his mind to follow Savery's example when leading his own men.

Savery came through the battle unscathed, but his brother Isaac was not impressed with his behaviour. Just a few days shy of his thirtieth birthday, Isaac, who commanded the Forty-Ninth as senior lieutenant-colonel, was also a large man, at least six feet two inches tall. Despite the rank, he was as inexperienced in combat as James FitzGibbon, and his first battle nearly proved his last.

The Forty-Ninth acquitted itself well, with Brock leading a charge that sent the enemy into retreat. But then a bullet hit him in the throat, stunning him. Fortunately, the impact of the bullet was diminished by the distance it had travelled and a heavy cotton handkerchief he had wrapped over his thick silk cravat as extra protection against the cold weather. In a letter to his older brother John, Brock wrote, "I got knocked down soon after the enemy began to retreat, but never quitted the field, and returned to my duty in less than half an hour."

As far as Isaac was concerned, it was perfectly acceptable to downplay his own close call, but his younger brother's recklessness was another matter. He scolded Savery, reminding him he had told him to stay away from the fighting unless Abercromby needed him. Savery replied with a grin, suggesting his brother mind his own business. "Tend to your regiment, Master Isaac." Although younger than Isaac, Savery definitely had a mind of his own. In fact, his independence of thought had forced him to resign from the Royal Navy after he had flouted regulations by signing a petition to end the practice of sending sailors to the masthead for long periods of time as a punishment.

What happened next between Isaac and Savery at Egmont-op-Zee is not recorded. Brothers in the twenty-first century might have punched each other in the arm, hugged, or gone for drinks. Brothers in the nineteenth century likely did something similar. The missing details don't matter. What the exchange between the young Brock brothers hints at is the dynamics of the family that produced brave soldiers and successful businessmen, including the man who would eventually be hailed as the saviour of Upper Canada.

Long established on the English Channel island of Guernsey by the mid-eighteenth century, the Brocks were a wealthy and genteel family with considerable local influence. John Brock, born in 1729, had been a midshipman in the Royal Navy. In 1758 he married Elizabeth de Lisle, whose father had been lieutenant bailiff of Guernsey. One of their sons, Daniel, would serve as bailiff—chief justice and president of the legislature—from 1821 to 1842.

Elizabeth and John produced fourteen children, ten of

whom grew to adulthood. Isaac, born on October 6, 1769, was the eleventh child and eighth son. Five of his elder brothers, John, Ferdinand, Daniel, William, and Frederick, would all survive to manhood and, when Isaac was born, their ages ranged from ten to one. Although they all eventually left home for schooling or careers, their presence meant Isaac grew up in a boisterous, predominantly masculine atmosphere that would shape his character. Known among the extended family for his gentleness, Isaac was determinedly studious, often shutting himself in a room for hours to read. But he was also athletic, the "best boxer and boldest swimmer" among his schoolmates, and grew into a strong youth who was very tall for his age.

In 1779, at the age of ten, young Isaac was sent to a boarding school in Southampton, England. His father had died at forty-eight in 1777 and, two years later, his brother Ferdinand was killed at nineteen while defending Baton Rouge, Louisiana, from the Spanish during the American Revolutionary War. While he must have grieved over those losses, Isaac's surviving brothers helped fill the gap in his life, providing affection, guidance, and examples for him to follow.

In 1783, Isaac spent some time improving his French skills under the tutelage of a Protestant French pastor in Rotterdam, Netherlands. In March 1785, using funds borrowed from his brother William, a merchant banker in

London, Isaac bought an ensign's commission in the Eighth Regiment of Foot (King's Regiment), where his eldest brother, John, had just purchased a captaincy. Buying commissions in the army was a widespread practice at the time, and while it did lead to some abuses, it was generally accepted as a way in which promising young men could rise quickly through the ranks without waiting for the cumbersome bureaucracy of the army to give them promotions.

Isaac's first assignment was garrison duty in England. In 1790, again using money borrowed from William, he purchased a lieutenant's commission. With Britain on the brink of war with Napoleon Bonaparte, the government authorized the creation of new regiments. Isaac took advantage of the situation to raise an independent company and was rewarded for this service with a promotion to captain. After a brief time stationed in Guernsey and Jersey, he transferred to the Forty-Ninth Regiment of Foot, still with the rank of captain.

A little while after joining the Forty-Ninth, twenty-one-year-old Captain Brock was challenged to a duel by another officer who made a habit of drawing others into disputes. Typically, duelists stood back to back, paced off a dozen steps each, then turned and fired. Whether they hit their opponents depended on their skill and the quality of their weapons, but the larger a man was, the more likely he would be wounded or killed. And the man who had challenged

Sir Isaac Brock, portrait by J. Hudson

Brock was a skilled marksman! Realizing his size put him at a disadvantage, Isaac accepted the challenge on one condition—he and his opponent would each hold one end of a handkerchief and fire from that distance. Unwilling to risk certain injury and possible death, the opponent backed down and soon left the regiment in disgrace.

In 1791, the Forty-Ninth was stationed in Jamaica and Barbados, a mixed blessing for the soldiers. While the tropics were exotically beautiful, they were also full of diseases to which Europeans had little immunity. Food also spoiled more rapidly and water supplies became contaminated more quickly because of the heat. Like many of his comrades-in-arms, including his own cousin, Brock contracted a fever. The cousin died but Isaac was more fortunate. Private James Dobson, his servant, tenderly nursed him until he was out of danger. As soon as he was fit to travel, Brock returned to Guernsey to recover his health.

Once he was fit, he returned to duty and continued his ascent through the ranks by purchasing more commissions. By 1797, the year his mother died, he was lieutenant-colonel of the regiment and found his predecessor had left regimental affairs in disarray. There were shortages of clothing and equipment and, worse, the regiment was not at full strength. One of Brock's first tasks was to put things back in order, a goal he accomplished so well that he was praised by Frederick, Duke of York, second son of King George III and commander-in-chief of the British army.

At this point, Great Britain was at war. In the aftermath of the French Revolution, Britain and other European countries had tried to restore the French monarchy by force.

Although there would be interim periods of peace, the rise of Napoleon Bonaparte, and the "little corporal's" ambitious plan to conquer Europe, locked Britain and its allies into years of costly fighting. Yet Brock remained far from the theatres of war. Brock had been born in the same year as both Napoleon Bonaparte and the man who would eventually defeat him, Arthur Wellesley, Duke of Wellington. Given his character, Brock likely found it ironic that he spent so much time sitting on the sidelines. But the experience he gained, including that of recruiting soldiers for the war effort, would prove useful later in his career.

Brock's actions at Egmont-op-Zee in 1799 proved he could lead men in battle. He also proved himself away from combat through his administration of the regiment and his firm but fair discipline. Vigorous, athletic, brave, and gregarious, Brock was also deeply concerned about the welfare of his men, and it made him extremely popular with many of them. Maybe too much so, as one incident in Jersey in 1800 revealed. While Brock was temporarily away from the regiment, command fell to junior lieutenant-colonel Roger Hale Sheaffe. Six years older than Brock, Sheaffe was born in Boston, Massachusetts, son of the deputy collector of customs. When his father died, Sheaffe's mother opened a boarding house that became the headquarters of Earl Hugh Percy, future Duke of Northumberland, during the American Revolutionary War. The earl took an interest in young Roger, made sure he was educated, and purchased commissions in the army for him. Sheaffe's military career proceeded nicely, and at one time he acted as an emissary for John Graves Simcoe, first lieutenant-governor of Upper Canada. According to Simcoe, Sheaffe was "A gentleman of great discretion, incapable of any intemperate or uncivil conduct." But James FitzGibbon saw another side of him. Although he was the best teacher FitzGibbon ever knew, he was also a "martinet and scold" who was always cursing his men. "His offensive language often marred his best efforts," FitzGibbon recalled. While such behaviour was not unusual at the time, in FitzGibbon's opinion it had a negative impact on the troops and undermined morale. Eventually, the Duke of York would introduce regulations to limit abusive language, but not until after Sheaffe had temporarily replaced Brock.

The men were so disgusted by Sheaffe's harsh treatment and foul language that when Brock reappeared on the parade grounds after returning to duty they gave him three rousing cheers.

A lesser man might have accepted the tribute with a smile, but Brock immediately recognized that it was a breach of military discipline that could undermine the authority of Sheaffe and other unpopular officers. Chiding his men for the outburst, he ordered them confined to barracks for a week.

The following year, both Brock and Sheaffe were with the

Forty-Ninth at Copenhagen, Denmark. Although Russia was allied with France at the time of the battle at Egmont-op-Zee, Czar Paul had later coordinated an arrangement with Sweden and Denmark, creating the League of Armed Neutrality. One of the main purposes of the alliance was to allow the three countries to continue trading with Napoleonic France. The British considered this unacceptable, and in early 1801 a fleet was organized to attack Copenhagen and dissolve the league. More than 120 ships under command of Admiral Sir Hyde Parker set sail on March 12, 1801.

Copenhagen harbour was protected by a number of ships and hulks floating outside the entrance, as well by the Trekroner Fort, which was armed with sixty-eight heavy guns. Typically, an attack on the fort would have been handled by marines, but none were available for this expedition. Instead, the army was called upon, and a company of the Sixtieth Royal Americans, as well as the Forty-Ninth Regiment, accompanied the fleet to Denmark. Brock was assigned to lead the land forces in the assault and sailed aboard the *Ganges*, while his men were distributed among seven other vessels.

The battle got underway around 10 a.m. on the morning of April 2, 1801, and raged for more than five hours. By 1:30 p.m., three of the ships carrying members of the Forty-Ninth—*Agamemnon, Russell,* and *Bellona*—had all run aground. Meanwhile, Horatio Nelson, already a celebrated war hero who had lost one arm and the sight in one eye during previous battles, continued to bombard the enemy. Unable to see Nelson's ship through the smoke, Admiral Parker, a cautious commander at the best of times, concluded that Nelson might be no longer making any headway but unable to withdraw without express orders. To give him the option of an honourable retreat, Parker commanded his flag captain to signal Nelson accordingly. But Nelson was not inclined to leave the battle. "You know, Foley," he said to his own flag captain, "I only have one eye—I have the right to be blind sometimes." He then raised the telescope to his sightless eye and said, "I really do not see the signal."

A short time later, the Danish defence began to crumble, fighting ceased, and the process of negotiating a truce began. Brock's regiment had not been needed to attack the enemy, but the Forty-Ninth still suffered thirteen killed and forty-one wounded, mostly aboard the *Monarch.* Savery Brock also had another close call. Like Isaac, Savery was aboard the *Ganges,* where, as a former naval officer, he helped by manning one of the guns. As he was pointing it towards the enemy, grapeshot tore off his hat, knocking him to the deck. Isaac was close enough to see it and exclaimed, "Ah! Poor Savery is dead!" The words were barely out of his mouth when Savery was back on his feet and firing the gun as though nothing had happened.

James FitzGibbon, who had been taken prisoner in Holland but later released, escaped the Battle of

Copenhagen physically unharmed. But his youthful pride almost sabotaged his career one morning after that battle. While aboard the *Elephant*, FitzGibbon was summoned to the deck by Colonel Hutchinson. He took longer getting there than the colonel anticipated, and Hutchinson scolded him loudly, threatening to court martial him and reduce him to the ranks. FitzGibbon brooded about the rebuke all day, then approached Hutchinson, saluted, and told him that, since he could not perform his duty as a sergeant with-out criticism, he wished to be demoted to private. Startled and angry, Hutchinson gave him his wish but the next day questioned FitzGibbon again. Likely suspecting the young man had been drinking, the colonel asked if he remembered what he had said the day before. When FitzGibbon assured him that he did and that he would not change his mind, Hutchinson confirmed the demotion and dismissed him in disgust.

FitzGibbon remained a private while the fleet patrolled the Baltic and charted its shallow waters. At the end of August, the Forty-Ninth returned to England, disembarking at various ports, then marching to headquarters at Colchester. When the men assembled there, Brock greeted them, thanking them for their bravery and good conduct while stationed on their separate vessels. A little later, having spoken to FitzGibbon's colonel, Brock questioned FitzGibbon about his demotion aboard the *Elephant*. He was particularly concerned about whether FitzGibbon had meant to insult Colonel Hutchinson. FitzGibbon assured him that he had not. He had felt humiliated by being censured before two officers who had previously shown him consideration, and, because he considered Hutchinson "an angry officer" he was convinced he would never get ahead under Hutchinson's command. So he had requested the demotion to save himself further grief.

Brock, who realized FitzGibbon's potential, persuaded the young man to go to Hutchinson and give him a full explanation. After this was done, Hutchinson personally approached Brock and asked that FitzGibbon be reinstated as sergeant, and it was done.

Six months later, on March 25, 1802, the Peace of Amiens was signed, ending the war between Britain and France. As Britain reduced the strength of its army and navy, the Forty-Ninth was ordered to service in Canada.

Chapter 2
Posted to Canada

When Lieutenant-Colonel Isaac Brock landed at Quebec City in August 1802, he was nearly thirty-three. Loved and respected by his men, trusted by his superiors, he had already spent more than half his life in the army. Although his combat experience was limited, there was no doubt about his courage, his initiative, or his leadership ability. As William Hamilton Merritt, who served in the Upper Canadian militia during the War of 1812, would later write, Brock was "active, brave, vigilant and determined" and "had a peculiar faculty of attaching all parties and people to his person." Because of those skills, within ten years—counting almost from the day of his arrival—he would become commander-in-chief of the army in Canada, acting head of the government of Upper Canada, and a celebrated war hero.

But first he had to wrestle with the realities of life in mainland Canada. Quebec City, where he landed, was a key point in the defence of British North America, guarding the St. Lawrence River and the Great Lakes beyond. Land travel was difficult in the early nineteenth century, even in Lower Canada, which had been settled for two hundred years. When it rained, roads typically turned into a muddy mess where wagons and draft animals got bogged down. In winter, if conditions were right, horse-drawn sleighs could move rapidly across the frozen surfaces. But winter was just as likely to bring heavy snowfalls that the wind blew into impassable drifts. In contrast, as long as the waters were open, the St. Lawrence and the Great Lakes provided quick and comparatively cheap routes for the movement of men and supplies. They were also the key to the defence of the country in case of war.

Although the Peace of Amiens was still in effect when Brock reached Canada, it was an uneasy peace. Few doubted that it would be only a matter of time before Napoleon Bonaparte's ambition brought France into direct conflict with Britain again. Meanwhile, relations between Britain and the United States remained strained. Although trade was brisk between the two countries, political differences constantly threatened to erupt into a full-blown war. American forces had invaded Canada in 1775, occupied Montreal, and laid siege to Quebec before being repelled by the British army.

Sir Isaac Brock, portrait by J. W. L. Forster

Twenty-seven years later, there was still a segment of the American population that viewed the conquest of Canada as unfinished business.

Complicating matters was the nature of the Canadian population. Lower Canada, with a population of about 330,000, had three French-Canadians for every one English-Canadian, and a significant number of those English-speakers were American-born Loyalists deeply resented by the original settlers of the province. At the same time, the English-speaking residents of the province, especially government officials, worried about the loyalties of the francophones, especially after the French Revolution of 1789. The Roman Catholic Church made it clear that it could not support a regime that had overthrown the French monarchy, and that French Canada's loyalties rightly belonged to Britain. But there were still fears that French Canadians would eventually try to avenge the conquest of 1759.

Upper Canada was much more sparsely populated, with about 80,000 residents stretched out along a vast frontier within a few miles of the American border. Many of them—perhaps as many as 40 per cent—had been born in the United States, and not all of them felt any particular loyalty to the British Crown. In the aftermath of the American Revolution, John Graves Simcoe, first lieutenant-governor of Upper Canada, had realized that Americans, unlike settlers from Britain, had all the skills needed to develop wild land.

Simcoe's offer of generous land grants lured many people of the United States north, some of whom arrived with large extended families and republican views.

Brock had to absorb all this upheaval and more as he carried out his duties, first in Quebec, then in Montreal, and, by the summer of 1803, in Upper Canada. Brock and part of the Forty-Ninth were stationed at York (now Toronto), with the grenadier company in a blockhouse at the east end of the muddy provincial capital while the remainder of the troops were billeted in the garrison at Fort York. As the summer progressed, many of the grenadiers fell ill with ague and fever, undoubtedly carried by mosquitoes in the swampy lands along the Don River close to the blockhouse. Brock, always concerned about his men's well-being, dealt with the problem by transferring the grenadiers to the garrison, even though accommodations there were barely more tolerable.

The Peace of Amiens collapsed in May 1803 and Napoleon readied his army and navy for an invasion of England. With Britain and France now once more at war, relations with the United States took a downturn. As a result, part of the Forty-Ninth regiment was stationed along the Niagara River, which formed the border between Canadian and American territories. Some of the men were at Fort Erie, where the river flowed out of Lake Erie, some were above Niagara Falls at Chippawa, and others were well below the falls at Fort George, close to the town of Newark (now

Niagara-on-the-Lake) at Lake Ontario.

Roger Sheaffe was put in charge of the garrison at Fort George, and once again his personality and style of leadership created some serious problems—not that Sheaffe can be entirely blamed for the dramatic and dangerous developments of the summer of 1803. Despite the threat of war, there really was not much to occupy troops stationed in Upper Canada. When drills, patrols, and guard duties were done, the men would sometimes fish or hunt, providing they had the permission of their commanding officer, or would spend whatever time they had off duty at a local tavern. Heavy drinking was widespread, leading to fistfights, thievery, and other mischief. But boredom also took its toll, especially for soldiers who were less than content with the conditions in the military. At the Niagara garrisons in particular, the United States, just a short distance across the river, tempted soldiers who dreamed of possibilities not available to them in this army or back home in Britain. There might be land, better wages, and adventure. For the Irish, whose endemic poverty often had forced them into military service, the United States had a special appeal. The Americans had thrown off the yoke of British rule, something segments of the Irish population had repeatedly tried and failed to do, as recently as 1798. Desertions were frequent.

Late one August night in 1803, James FitzGibbon, by

now a sergeant-major, wakened Brock to inform him that three sentries from the Forty-Ninth at York had deserted, along with two other men from the regiment and a corporal from the Forty-First. The six had stolen a boat and headed across Lake Ontario, likely destined for Fort Niagara on the American side of the Niagara River. Brock ordered FitzGibbon to gather twelve men and launch a boat, and, shortly after midnight, set off with them across the lake. When they reached Fort George at dawn, Brock sent Lieutenant Edward Cheshire and a party of men across the river to look for deserters on the American side. It was a rash act, a violation of American neutrality at a time when international relations were precarious, but Brock was willing to take the risk. Meanwhile, Brock himself took a group of men to look along the river on the Canadian side.

Cheshire and his men, possibly helped by a native scout, found the deserters and brought them back to Fort George. They were imprisoned pending trial.

Perhaps it was the summer heat, perhaps the boredom, perhaps rumours about the punishment that awaited the men once they were court-martialled. Whatever the cause, soon after the deserters were captured something far more serious was uncovered. One of the soldiers, possibly a Private John Daly, at Knox's Tavern in Newark, overheard some of his comrades plotting a mutiny. The plan was to murder Roger Sheaffe, imprison other officers, steal ammunition, and desert to the American side.

Daly immediately reported what he had heard to Roger Sheaffe, who consulted his officers. When he learned that the troops were indeed seriously disgruntled and that a mutiny was a distinct possibility, Sheaffe was in a quandary. This was not only beyond anything he had dealt with in his years as an officer, but it was also, he was wise enough to realize, something he was incapable of handling with both the efficiency and the delicacy required. He hastily scrawled a note to Brock, then entrusted it to a captain with the Provincial Marine with instructions to get it to the lieutenant-colonel as soon as possible.

The boat set off in the afternoon. Brock received the note that evening and immediately headed back across the lake, accompanied by his trusty sergeant-major, James FitzGibbon. Heavy winds made the crossing arduously slow, delaying the arrival of Brock and his party until late the next morning.

According to one account, Brock ordered the boat anchored below Newark, told FitzGibbon to stay put until summoned, then approached the fort alone. When he arrived, the men were at dinner. Stationing trusted officers at the doors, Brock entered and, one by one, handcuffed the offenders.

Whether that story is true, or one of the many legends that have been attached to Brock over the years, the plotters

were definitely arrested. With the eight men who had deserted earlier, they were sent to Quebec to await trial. In the
meantime, Brock probed into the conditions that had led to
the near-mutiny and discovered how Sheaffe had contributed to the situation.

Fishing and hunting were two of the few harmless
pastimes that soldiers could pursue. They also had the
advantage of allowing men to augment their humdrum and
sometimes unpalatable rations. Sheaffe had refused to allow
them to fish unless dressed in full uniform—which meant
their white uniform trousers became easily soiled. He also
refused to allow them to use their army-issue weapons for
hunting, even if they paid for their own shot and powder. Nor
had he changed the behaviour that had created so much dis-
satisfaction among his men when the regiment was stationed
in Jersey. Sheaffe still cursed them and punished them for
relatively minor infractions with demotions, floggings, and
solitary confinement.

Brock was in a dilemma. On the one hand, he genuinely
liked Roger Sheaffe, enjoyed his company, and appreciated
his abilities as a soldier. On the other, he realized Sheaffe
was a perfectionist who completely lacked the common
touch that Brock himself had in abundance. "He did not
sufficiently study the character of the men," Brock observed
in his report to Lieutenant-Colonel James Green, secretary
to Peter Hunter, Upper Canada's lieutenant-governor. "His

ardent zeal made him sick with eagerness after perfection where it was not to be found." Because of his harsh discipline, Sheaffe made many enemies, who delighted in spreading rumours and exaggerating his perceived shortcomings. Brock was willing to admit his friend and brother-in-arms possessed "little knowledge of mankind," was at least partly to blame for the mutinous plot, and had "greatly fallen in the estimation of the men." But he could not completely condemn him. Instead, although he conceded that Sheaffe had made an "error in judgment," Brock stressed, "No man understands the duties of his profession better than Colonel Sheaffe." Believing the experience would force Sheaffe to change his behaviour, he recommended treating him with "the usual confidence." As far as Brock was concerned, the underlying problem was not Sheaffe's incompetence or lack of judgment, but rather the conditions prevalent at Fort George and "the temptations which are perpetually offered to the unwary soldier."

It was February 1804 when Brock penned his assessment of the whole situation, which had resulted in his transfer from Fort York to Fort George. Soon afterward, the final act in the drama of desertion and mutiny played out in Quebec. Of the twenty men arrested and sent to trial, one was acquitted. Nine men, seven of them from the Forty-Ninth, were transported for life. Another seven, one from the Forty-First and six from the Forty-Ninth, were sentenced to death and shot on March 2. Immediately before their execution, several of them declared that they would not have become involved in the plot had they remained under Brock's command.

The disgraceful demise of men with whom he had seen combat affected Brock deeply and he expressed his sorrow both publicly and privately. When news of the executions reached Fort George, he addressed the men, informing them of events and adding, "Since I have had the honour to wear the British uniform, I have never felt grief like this, as it pains me to think that any members of my regiment should have engaged in a conspiracy which has led to their being shot like so many dogs!" Brock's reaction, as much as the plotters' deaths, must have had a profound impact on his regiment.

Brock returned to Quebec in 1804, where he was placed in command of the garrison at Quebec City. Some time before his departure, he made the acquaintance of Robert Nichol, who was then running a store at Fort Erie. At that point, the business was struggling, which may have accounted for James FitzGibbon's assessment of Nichol as "a mean looking little Scotchman, who squinted very much," and kept a "Retail Store of Small Consideration." Nichol was unusually short and did squint, probably because he was terribly nearsighted. But twenty-three-year-old FitzGibbon, who was tall, extremely strong, and not bad-looking, may have been jealous of the attention his mentor was paying to the little

Scot. Nichol was a relative and erstwhile employee of Robert Hamilton, one of the richest men in Niagara and owner of a house that Elizabeth Simcoe, wife of the lieutenant-governor, had described as the finest in the province. Deeply embedded in the business community of Upper Canada, Nichol had connections from Detroit to Niagara and beyond, as well as a keen, analytical mind that would serve Brock well. Despite some genteel officers' prejudices against tradesmen such as Nichol, Brock valued Nichol's "zeal, prudence and intelligence," frequently inviting him to dinner at the officers' mess, where he tapped into his extensive knowledge about transportation and provisions.

After several months in Quebec, Brock returned to England on leave, partly to deal with some financial matters. While there he continued to think about the defence of Canada, including the problem of desertion. He discussed the matter with the Duke of York, suggesting that a battalion of veterans be raised for duty at the remote Canadian outposts. As far as he was concerned, these veterans were less likely to desert than the greener troops. In December 1806, the Tenth Royal Veterans Battalion was raised and was sent to Quebec in 1807.

Brock also looked at the possibility of raising a force from the residents of Glengarry County, in eastern Upper Canada. These were Roman Catholic Scots who had been forced out of their homeland by the Highland clearances.

Although Sir James Craig authorized the organization of the infantry, the officers were unable to obtain enough volunteers within the period of time stipulated just then. It was December 1811 before the Glengarry Light Infantry came into being.

Despite his concerns for the defence of Canada, Brock was longing to serve in Europe, where there were better chances for fame and glory. He had the connections, was highly regarded, and likely could have been sent to join Wellington's army. But his sense of duty, and perhaps the realization that he was one of the few officers who had a good grasp of Canadian conditions, persuaded him to cross the Atlantic once again in September 1806.

Many Americans had been calling for war since the spring. On April 25, a fifty-gun British ship, *Leander*, attempted to stop and inspect *Richard*, an American schooner about two miles off the coast of Shady Hook, New Jersey. Such inspections were routine. To undermine France's economy, the British had enacted laws forbidding the transportation of French trade goods by neutral vessels. American ships often ignored those laws and deeply resented the inspections.

When *Leander*'s commander ordered *Richard* to stop, her captain refused. *Leander* then fired a warning shot, but instead of flying harmlessly into the water the cannonball hit the *Richard*'s taffrail. The wood splintered, scattering in all directions and killing first mate John Pierce. *Richard*'s captain then permitted the inspection, but no contraband goods were found. When the ship got into New York City, Pierce's body was publicly displayed in the streets and news of the incident created considerable outrage against the British.

When Brock returned to Canada in the fall of 1806 he was the senior officer in the country and so was appointed commander-in-chief of all the forces, at least until Governor General Sir James Craig arrived in 1807. But, before that happened, yet another controversial incident involving British and American ships brought the two countries closer to the brink of war.

Chapter 3
Waiting for War

From September 1806, when he returned from England, until October 1807, when the new governor general, Sir James Craig, arrived, Brock was the highest-ranking military officer in the Canadas, as well as acting head of government. As both, Brock was responsible for defending the colonies in the event of war with the United States. As many military men before and since were aware, the key to an effective defence was control of the Great Lakes. And, given the comparatively small population in Upper Canada, continuing a strong alliance with the native people would be necessary. But, in the big picture, Upper Canada was expendable. Far more important, in the eyes of top British strategists, was the preservation of Halifax, Britain's most important naval station in North America, and, after that, Quebec City. The defence of both places would have to be done with a relatively small number of troops, both regulars and militia. As long as Napoleon and his supporters were keeping the British army and its allies busy in Europe, no men could be spared to wage an offensive war against the United States.

Brock kept himself busy repairing the fortress at Quebec, parts of which were crumbling into ruin. Finding the money and the men to carry out this task proved difficult, as the Lower Canadian government was less than cooperative, but it was accomplished. As he once told James FitzGibbon when the young sergeant failed to complete a difficult task, "By the Lord Harry, sir, do not tell me it is impossible. Nothing should be impossible for a soldier. The word impossible should not be found in a soldier's dictionary." Using a mixture of charm, persuasion, and persistence, Brock steered through the minefield of conflicting military and civilian priorities to do what he felt had to be done. He had trees and shrubs cleared away from the front of the fortress and also installed eight heavy guns. Locals referred to it as "Brock's Battery," but when Sir James Craig arrived, he decided the "King's Battery" would be a more appropriate name.

Before the fortress was completed, another crisis prompted more American demands for a declaration of war. Aside from looking for contraband cargo on American ships, the British navy frequently stopped American vessels in hopes of finding deserters, as well as British subjects who could be forced into service. Although the United States' system allowed for the naturalization of immigrants from Britain and other countries, the British view was that anyone born a British subject died a British subject. The opposing views created friction, especially when overzealous British officers seized sailors who had probably never set foot on British soil.

On June 22, 1807, the American frigate *Chesapeake* was off Hampton Roads, Virginia, when she passed some British ships still at anchor. One of them, *Leopard*, weighed anchor and pursued her. The *Chesapeake* stopped, and a British lieutenant boarded her and demanded the surrender of four deserters: William Ware, Daniel Martin, John Strachan, and Jenkin Ratford. James Barron, captain of the *Chesapeake*, refused. The lieutenant returned to *Leopard* and, using a loud-hailer, again demanded the men. Barron repeated his refusal and *Leopard* fired a warning shot at *Chesapeake*. When Barron remained unresponsive, *Leopard* fired three broadsides, killing three crewmen outright, mortally wounding another, and injuring fifteen more. *Chesapeake* was so severely damaged that Barron had to surrender. The men were taken to Halifax, where Ware, Martin, and Strachan were imprisoned. Ratford was charged with mutiny, desertion, and contempt, found guilty, and hanged from the yardarm on August 31.

Incensed, a number of Americans, especially pro-war

Republicans, claimed that the United States was "on the eve of war." It wasn't, but the emotional reaction created by the *Chesapeake* affair again underscored America's anti-British sentiments. By 1812, the slogan "free trade and sailors' rights" would emerge, summarizing what some believed were the causes for the war. What Americans conveniently forgot was that, in the process of enforcing its own restrictions on trade between 1803 and 1812, France seized approximately the same number of American ships as Britain did. The Americans, however, focused on Britain's perceived insults to America's national honour, on Britain's undermining of international trade, and on their conviction that the British were encouraging native peoples to attack frontier settlements in the United States. Added to this view was their notion that the United States was destined to occupy all of North America and to drive the British from the continent.

Not everyone believed war would come, but Isaac Brock was determined to be prepared. Aside from improving defences, he also paid attention to the red tape involved in running an army. When he found too many unexplained expenditures in the commissary department, he probed further. In the process, it was revealed that John Craigie, who had been commissary general since 1784, was diverting government funds for personal use. In 1808 Craigie was dismissed. Brock also insisted that the commissaries in Upper Canada send proper reports to Quebec or lose their jobs after he discovered that men attached to the Provincial Marine in Kingston had not been paid in seven months.

Even when not engaged with official duties, Brock kept himself busy. Because of his position, he was expected to attend various balls and social functions, which he generally enjoyed. While the social and cultural life of the colonies was a far cry from that of England and Europe, it was a welcome break from humdrum existence.

Brock enjoyed good food and drink, as well as comfortable surroundings. While he may have been perfectly capable of dealing with comparatively rough conditions on campaign or in foreign garrisons, his upbringing and his family's social position had accustomed him to the luxuries enjoyed by the gentry. An inventory of his effects taken after his death in 1812 includes numerous dishes, pots, pans, utensils, drinking glasses, plates, and decanters. Tablecloths, napkins, covers, curtains, and carpets were among his household goods, along with such furniture as a bedstead, more than a dozen chairs, several tables, and a writing desk. As for comestibles, he had well over a hundred bottles of wine, brandy, champagne, and beer, plus an assortment of preserves and condiments, including mustard, sugar, ketchup, pickles, and essence of lemon, all meant to enhance the flavour of his meals.

Obtaining the things he needed to be comfortable was not always easy in Canada, so Brock relied on his family to ship them from home. In July 1810, he wrote to thank his brother Irving for sending a number of items and to report that all had arrived safely "with the exception of the cocked hat, which has not been received—a most distressing circumstance, as, from the enormity of my head, I find the utmost difficulty in getting a substitute in this country." He had always been a big man, with an unusually large head, and, although he was still physically active, he had put on weight over the years. The military tunic he wore in 1812 measures 134.6 cm around the chest and 119.4 cm around the waist.

There is some evidence that the food and drink Brock enjoyed contributed to health problems. He was occasionally seen walking with a cane, which suggests that he may have suffered from gout. In a letter to his brother Irving in January 1811, Brock discussed the possibility of a trip to the spa in Ballston, New York, southwest of Saratoga Springs. He thought the mineral waters would be "serviceable." Although he reported he was feeling "infinitely better" he was unsure what was wrong, other than a lack of appetite and the need for a change. "At present," he told Irving, "I live very abstemiously and scarcely ever touch wine." His careful diet helped. Within a month he was feeling much better and cancelled the trip.

While he complained to Irving that he led an "uninteresting and insipid life," Brock possessed a library of about a hundred books, including military histories and two versions of the works of Shakespeare. The books were both a diversion and a means of improving his mind and his professional skills. He also enjoyed drawing, an accomplishment most gentlemen then were expected to possess.

Most gentlemen were also expected to marry. Many officers of Brock's age and rank were married. Brock was handsome—tall and fair, with blue-grey eyes and excellent teeth—he was charming, and he was powerful. He also enjoyed the company of women, sometimes asking members of his family to pass along his greetings to favourite female acquaintances. Some of his male friends encouraged him to take a wife, but there is no evidence that Brock was involved in any serious romance during his time in Canada.

What is clear is that, in spite of all his professional and social responsibilities, he kept up a steady correspondence with his extended family. Writing to one of his sisters-in-law on July 10, 1810, he reported that the arrival of Upper Canada's Lieutenant-Governor Francis Gore had given a "zest" to local social activities. "Races, country and water parties have occupied our time in a continued round of festivity. Such stimulus is highly necessary to keep our spirits afloat." He also asked to be remembered to his nieces Maria and Zelia Potenger, and promised if he could get "handsome skins" in the fall, he'd send them back to England so the girls could have muffs made from them.

Although he had no children of his own and his nieces

and nephews were an ocean away, Brock seems to have enjoyed youngsters. In 1810, after a Captain Ellis of the Forty-Ninth was drowned on his way home from Canada, Brock took his eight-year-old son into his home and cared for him like a son. There is also a story that Brock became friendly with an American doctor and his three young daughters, who often crossed the Niagara River to attend services at St. Mark's Church in Newark. On the Sunday before war was declared, the story goes, Brock insisted on embracing each girl in turn, before saying goodbye to their father with the sad comment that the next time they met it would be as enemies. Unless Brock was clairvoyant, the story is at least partly apocryphal—he had no way of knowing exactly when war would be declared. But the girls' memories of the fond farewell is likely true, reflecting Brock's affectionate nature.

With the arrival of Governor General Sir James Craig, Brock's duties diminished somewhat. At Craig's direction, he spent some time in Montreal, then returned to Quebec. But he was chafing at the inactivity and thought he might be more useful in Europe. Craig refused to let him go. He was too valuable, too well-informed about the Canadas. In the late summer of 1810, Craig made plans to send Brock to Upper Canada. This was particularly awkward for Brock, because he would be ordered back to Montreal if a higher-ranking officer arrived, but in the meantime would either have to bear the cost of transferring all his personal belongings to his new posting or be "miserably off" over the winter since so few luxuries were available in Upper Canada. He also expressed regret at the thought of leaving his "delightful garden" with its "abundance of melons and other good things." But there was no question of disobeying Craig's orders, and by September 1810 Brock was back at Fort George.

He stayed until the following June, then returned to Montreal to take command of the garrison there. In the interim, Sir James Craig still refused to consider Brock's request to leave, convinced he was crucial to the safety of the Canadas in the event of war. Craig himself was seriously ill and had been asking for permission to leave Canada since 1810. He would finally sail for England in June 1811. A few months before his departure, though, he offered to send Brock his favourite horse, Alfred, as a "legacy" and token of his esteem. In June, Craig sailed for England and died there the following January.

On June 4, 1811, prior to Craig's departure, Brock was promoted to the rank of major-general, as was Roger Sheaffe. Brock was now entitled to a small staff. The ability to delegate tasks to his staff lightened Brock's workload to some extent, but not for long. When Upper Canada's lieutenant-governor Sir Francis Gore returned to England on leave that fall, Craig's successor, Sir George Prevost, decided Brock was "the fittest person" to temporarily head the government of that province. Brock was scheduled to begin his new duties as president, or

Fort George, Niagara, 1812, drawing by Alfred Sandham

administrator, of Upper Canada on October 8.

On October 6, he marked his forty-second birthday. While he might have reason to congratulate himself on all that he had accomplished in his career, newspapers fresh from Britain brought news so painful that he later described the day as "the first truly gloomy birthday I have ever passed." Brock and Le Mesurier, his brother William's banking firm, had gone bankrupt in mid-July—one of the many businesses that had fallen victim to the economic crisis caused by Napoleon Bonaparte's sanctions against British goods. Worse news followed. When William had loaned Brock the money with which to purchase his army commissions, the amounts had been entered in the company's ledgers. In all likelihood, William was simply keeping careful records and had no intention of asking Isaac for repayment. But creditors were now involved, and as far as they were concerned, Brock owed them £3,000. In addition, William's financial situation had a ripple effect throughout the family, which caused considerable friction among the previously close-knit Brock tribe.

Brock wrote to Irving, who had been working with William, telling him that he would turn over his entire government salary of £1,000 per year, and asking Irving to either pay off his debt as quickly as possible or use the funds to assist the family. He also urged his brother not to say anything to William that would make him feel worse than he already did, and encouraged Irving to help heal the rift in the extended family.

Debt was a serious matter in the early nineteenth century, one that could not only tarnish a gentleman's reputation but also lead to imprisonment. Brock was obviously concerned to avoid such disgrace, both for himself and for his family, so he must have been somewhat reassured when William wrote to say that, while the creditors would expect repayment, in his opinion they would not take any immediate action against Isaac as long as it was evident that he did intend to honour his debt. He then confided that a Mr. Ellice, lately arrived from Canada, had learned that Brock owed money, inquired about the details, then promised that if Brock couldn't pay, he would. In addition, William reported, Ellice stated that Isaac was "so beloved in Canada that you would not want friends who would feel pleasure in assisting you to any amount, if necessary."

Brock was still hoping for a chance to fight in Europe, and correspondence from various contacts suggested there was a distinct possibility this could be arranged, especially if someone could be found to replace him as commander and administrator of Upper Canada. Roger Sheaffe was a likely candidate, and the prospect must have been tempting. But now Brock could not afford to lose the extra £1,000, and this fact, as well as a sense of duty, probably influenced his decision when he was offered a posting to Europe early in 1812. On February 12, 1812, he formally requested permission to remain in Upper Canada.

He may have regretted his decision when he dealt with the Upper Canada legislature. As a soldier, Brock had a solid grasp on what was needed for the defence of the province. He had, in fact, outlined his plan to Prevost in December 1811, predicting that the Niagara Peninsula would be the main target if Americans declared war, stressing that Fort Amherstburg needed to be reinforced, that Lakes Erie and Huron needed to be patrolled by British ships, and that Kingston, a crucial link in the communications chain with Lower Canada, had to be protected. Brock was in favor of attacking both Detroit and

Michilimackinac to secure those two key points at the west end of the province. But Prevost, who responded on Christmas Eve, again urged caution and confided that he did not expect a declaration of war from the Americans but only "repeated petty aggressions from our neighbours."

Whether Prevost's prediction would come true remained to be seen. In the meantime, Brock planned to do everything possible to ready the province for a war. But dealing with the Legislature proved difficult. There was considerable difference of opinion, especially among the elected members of the Legislative Assembly. There was a certain reluctance to spend money needlessly. And there was a hypersensitivity displayed by many elected representatives who felt their rights and privileges were being trampled. Brock hoped to get the legislature to agree to a suspension of *habeas corpus,* which would allow for quick arrests and indefinite incarceration for those suspected of treason and other crimes. He also wanted changes to the *Militia Act,* which, among other things, would allow for the creation of flank companies who would train six days a month instead of a single day of the year, which was the existing standard for the Upper Canadian militia. The Legislature refused to comply on the suspension of *habeas corpus,* agreed to the changes in the *Militia Act,* but did not vote any funds to support the militia.

And then there was a tempest in a teapot involving Robert Nichol, the storekeeper Brock had befriended at Fort

Erie, and who had compiled for him an extremely useful list of resources in Upper Canada, including livestock available in various districts. Nichol had relocated to Dover, on Lake Erie, around 1808 and was now, in the words of Anna Powell, doyenne of York society, "a wealthy young merchant miller." In 1810, Nichol was one of three men appointed as road commissioners in London District. Because of various delays and lack of communication, it appeared that Nichol had misappropriated £300 of public funds. He had not, and had the documentation to prove it, but was so offended by the accusation that he complained loudly and publicly about MLAs who had raised the issue. Members of the Legislative Assembly, among them Joseph Willcocks, retaliated by tabling a motion that accused Nichol of making false and malicious statements about members of the house and breaching the privilege of members. His arrest was ordered and deputy sergeant-at-arms Stephen Jarvis was sent to Dover to seize Nichol and transport him to the drafty log building that served as York's jail. Fortunately, Nichol had influential friends and quickly secured his release, thanks to a writ of *habeas corpus* issued by Chief Justice Thomas Scott. But Scott's actions infuriated the legislature, who immediately charged the judge with breaching their privileges, then complained to Brock and asked him to bring the matter to the attention of the Prince Regent in England.

What they had not counted on was Brock's loyalty to his

friend and his disgust with the Assembly. On March 9, in a letter to the governor general, Brock wrote, "The inordinate power assumed by the House of Assembly is truly alarming and ought to be resisted." In his opinion, the action against Nichol stemmed from political rivalry and jealousy. Nichol was "a gentleman of strict probity, education, and ardent loyalty" whose arrest was "a wanton act of oppression" that had "greatly alarmed the most thinking part of the community." Ultimately, the fracas did not harm Nichol, who was elected MLA for Norfolk a few months later, but it did underscore the pettiness and vindictiveness that characterized some of the actions of the legislature. And one wonders if anyone contemplated the irony inherent in the Nichol controversy. Had the timing been slightly different, and had Brock been able to persuade the legislature to suspend *habeas corpus*, Nichol might have languished in jail indefinitely.

As a result of the legislation passed in early 1812, the various militia companies of Upper Canada were empowered to form flank companies that would train six days a month, an important step towards readying the defence of the province. Brock also looked at the issue of supplying troops with food, which would plague the military throughout the war.

At the beginning of the nineteenth century, armies in the field were expected to live off the land. This was possible in long-settled countries, at least in the absence of crop failures or an enemy's scorched-earth policy. But Upper Canada was still a frontier that had only recently begun to export surpluses of wheat and flour. As early as February 1812, Brock expressed fears that contractors from Lower Canada would corner the market on Upper Canadian flour with the aim of selling it back to the commissariat at exorbitant prices. Ensuring a steady supply of meat was also problematic. Because adequate feed for livestock was not always available, Upper Canadians sometimes had difficulty supplying their own needs. In addition, the province had to import all the salt it required for preserving the pork and beef that would be used for army rations. Robert Nichol's report provided a snapshot of what was available and allowed for the implementation of various measures that would preserve or increase the food supply. (Ironically, a certain amount of meat consumed by British troops and militia during the war would come from the enemy, as New Englanders continued to sell cattle to Lower Canada. Meanwhile, American grain was being shipped across the Atlantic to feed British troops in the Iberian peninsula.)

In addition to attempting to ensure an adequate food supply, Brock needed to win the support of the native people of Upper Canada. This task proved to be far more complicated than anticipated, especially where the Six Nations of the Grand River were concerned. Having supported the British during the American Revolution, the Six Nations had lost much of their land in the United States. In compensation,

Governor Frederick Haldimand had granted a huge tract on either side of the Grand River, which flows into Lake Erie. Led by Joseph Brant, a large segment of the Six Nations had settled on the tract, near the site of modern Brantford. As the years passed, they came into conflict with government policies about the distribution and sale of land. Brant and others felt that it was acceptable for them to sell Six Nations property and use the profits for the good of the community. The government's stance was that it alone was empowered to sell native lands. Meanwhile, certain agents of the British Indian Department sold land and pocketed the profits. In the spring of 1812, when Brock visited the Six Nations of the Grand to discuss their support in the event of war, he found them unwilling to make a commitment. Brant had been dead since 1807, and while his protegé, John Norton, was willing to support Brock's request, other leaders wanted certain conditions fulfilled first. They demanded the settlement of land claims and asked for a guarantee that the British would support the tribes in the U.S. midwest in their fight against Americans who were steadily encroaching on their territory. Brock was unable to satisfy either demand. Dealing with land claims was beyond his authority and it was not British policy to support attacks on the United States as long as the two nations were officially at peace.

To further complicate the situation, the Six Nations of the Grand were visited by delegates from the Six Nations who had remained in the United States. Invoking family ties and their common culture, the visitors urged neutrality, but there were some from the Grand who suspected the visitors were acting on behalf of the American government. One man from the Grand River warned that the Americans would destroy the Iroquois still living in the United States, making them "slaves like the Negroes." "The President wants you to lie still and hold down your heads," he added, "but I am a Mohawk. I will paint my face and be a man and fight Yankees as long as I live." Yet, in spite of these spirited words, the Six Nations of the Grand still would not promise their support.

In early June 1812, yet another delegation was sent from the United States, but this time Brock would not allow them to travel to the Grand River. Instead, the meeting was held in Queenston. Brock asked John Norton to send "reliable" representatives, but once again the talks were inconclusive, even though one speaker from the Grand River declared eloquently that the Six Nations living in Canada had already tied themselves to the fate of the British.

Unfortunately, those inspiring words did not accurately reflect the reality. The Six Nations remained divided, creating no end of frustration for Brock. On the one hand, he understood their anger about unsettled land claims and did what he could to help, arranging for the long-delayed interest due on land sales to be paid to them. Through reading and his own life experiences he had absorbed enough

Enlightenment philosophy to be able to see natives as human beings interested in the common human goals of "life, liberty, and the pursuit of happiness" so famously enshrined in the American Declaration of Independence. In fact, he would draw on those ideas to defend native participation in the war in a declaration of his own later that summer. But he was still very much a man of his culture, who could not come to grips with the huge differences between Europeans and natives. He described them as "a fickle race," thought the Six Nations' decision to remain neutral was audacious, and, in August 1812, when he felt the situation in Upper Canada was "extremely perilous," actually suggested that the best method of ending the problems with the natives would be to remove them from their land along the Grand River and exile them to the West. Fortunately, no one took his suggestion seriously.

While Brock dealt with various preparations for war, American politicians were debating the question with considerable fervour. In general, Republicans were in favour of war, especially those representing constituencies in the south and west. In the American legislature, just under a dozen "war hawks," led by the eloquent and determined Henry Clay, were the most vocal advocates of a declaration of war. As speaker of the House of Representatives, Clay had a huge edge that enabled him to interpret House rules to his advantage, or to pack key committees with his supporters. Day by day, they inched the United States towards a declaration of war.

When the vote finally came it was, in the words of historian Donald F. Hickey, "the closest vote on any formal declaration of war in American history." In the House of Representatives, seventy-nine voted for war, forty-nine against. The margin was even narrower in the Senate, where the vote was nineteen to thirteen in favour. On June 18, President James Madison signed the war bill, which was proclaimed the following day. Britain and the United States were officially at war.

Chapter 4
The Road to Detroit

With most of the British army occupied in Europe, and facing only a small Canadian population that included many immigrants from the United States, about 1,200 regular soldiers in Upper Canada, and an untried militia, the Americans were confident that they could easily win the war. In early August, former president Thomas Jefferson wrote, "The acquisition of Canada this year, as far as the neighborhood of Quebec, will be a mere matter of marching and will give us the experience for the attack of Halifax the next, and the final expulsion of England from the American continent." As it turned out, Canada would be much harder to conquer than he expected, and in the first weeks of the war it seemed that the Americans' lack of preparation and poor communications would scuttle their plans.

Before even the telegraph, alerting the military and the populace about a declaration of war took days, sometimes weeks. Brock did not receive official notification of the Americans' declaration until early July. Fortunately, business-men seemed to have a better grasp on the need for speed. Fur trader John Jacob Astor sent word to associates in Niagara, who passed the news along to Brock on June 26.

For months, Brock had been planning his strategy and knew one of the first things he had to do was secure Fort Mackinac on Michilimackinac Island. At the narrow passage between Lakes Michigan and Huron, it was a strategically important outpost guarding access to the rich fur country of the northwest, and the Americans had it. But, despite its importance, no one in Washington had thought to alert Lieutenant Porter Hanks.

Brock had no way of knowing that Hanks was unaware of the declaration of war when he wrote to Captain Charles Roberts, then in command of a post at St. Joseph Island, 80 km to the south. His instructions were clear. Roberts was to attack Michilimackinac immediately.

News of the declaration of war and Brock's instructions reached Roberts on July 3. There were certain obstacles to carrying out the orders. Roberts's command consisted of four dozen soldiers—three men from the Royal Regiment of Artillery and forty-five from the Tenth Royal Veteran Battalion—but they were hardly fit for battle after months at a remote frontier outpost. According to Roberts, they were "so debilitated, and worn down by unconquerable drunkenness, that neither the fear of punishment, the love of fame or the honour of their Country" would motivate them. Fortunately, Robert Dickson had arrived at St. Joseph around the end of June. Brother of Niagara businessmen Thomas and William Dickson and a cousin of Robert Nichol, Dickson was also known as Mascotapah, "the Red-Haired Man." He had lived among the natives for many years, and had been married to a Sioux woman since 1797. Shortly before the declaration of war, Brock had sent him a confidential message asking him to recruit men to support the British. On June 18, unaware of the American declaration that day, Dickson responded that he had gathered between 250 and 300 supporters and would take them immediately to St. Joseph Island. By mid-July, the place was crowded. Along with Dickson's warriors there were 180 employees of the North West Company and 300 Ottawa and Ojibwa summoned by John Askin Jr., another member of Dickson's extended family, who was serving as storekeeper and translator for the Indian Department at St. Joseph.

In the meantime, because Sir George Prevost was still urging caution in hopes of a quick, diplomatic end to the war, Brock uncharacteristically changed his orders and sent a letter to Roberts telling him not to attack Mackinac. But the warriors and voyageurs at St. Joseph were eager to engage the enemy, and there was always the possibility that the

Americans might mount an attack of their own. When Brock sent another letter telling Roberts to use his own discretion and "adopt the most prompt and effectual measures," the next step was clear. If he was to have any chance of taking Mackinac, Roberts had to act while the native warriors and North West Company men were still around to support his ragtag troops.

On July 16, Roberts's force of regulars, fur company employees, and native warriors piled into canoes, bateaux, and the North West Company brig, *Caledonia*, bound for Mackinac. They took along two six-pounder guns. When they reached the island at 3 a.m., one of the guns was landed and towed to a spot overlooking the fort. Meanwhile, the civilian population of the island was quietly rounded up and confined in an abandoned distillery.

Porter Hanks woke up to see the British gun aiming directly at his fort, and learned that war had been declared. Hanks was prepared to fight the enemy, but, like Roberts's troops, his men had grown soft in the remote outpost. Worse, the presence of more than a hundred native warriors on the enemy side frightened the Americans. Hanks surrendered. He and his men were paroled—sent home after they promised not to take up arms again unless formally exchanged as prisoners of war. Three British deserters who had been living on the island were taken into custody. Roberts then was able to report to Brock that the strategic gateway to the northwest

Portrait of Sir George Prevost, c. 1810

was securely under British-Canadian control. For Brock, the satisfaction that victory brought was tempered with sadness. James Dobson, an old servant who had nursed Brock back to health in the Caribbean, had just died after a long illness. Always kind-hearted and solicitous, Brock had visited him every day when possible and had made sure that Dobson received the very best care.

On the same day that Roberts set out for Mackinac, British-Canadian troops encountered American invaders at the Canard River, north of Amherstburg. The invasion had actually begun before war was declared, at the instigation of General William Hull, commander of the U.S. Army of the Northwest and governor of the Michigan territory. Hull was a veteran of the American Revolution, a Yale-trained lawyer known for his love of pompous speeches and fine clothing ornamented with gold braid and black feathers. While he had served with distinction during the Revolution and went on to a political career, he was a quarrelsome man who did not get along with other officers appointed to invade Canada during the War of 1812. Hull was also past his prime, having suffered a stroke in 1811 that made him mumble and drool at times. In addition, he was morbidly afraid of natives, who were most of the population in the territory he governed.

Despite his shortcomings, Hull was sufficiently determined and influential to convince President James Madison of the strategic sense of an invasion near Amherstburg, on the Detroit River. Conventional wisdom dictated an attack on Montreal from a base near Lake Champlain, in upper New York State, or an invasion of the Niagara Peninsula. But Hull argued that securing the Detroit area was vital. Most of the residents there were former French-Canadians who stayed on the American side after the territory west of the river was ceded to the U.S. in 1796 under Jay's Treaty. Because these settlers still had strong ties to family and friends on the Canadian side of the border, Hull believed it was essential to establish a strong American presence on both sides of the river. A successful invasion would both keep the French-Canadians on the American side loyal to the U.S. while discouraging resistance from those on the Canadian side, and, Hull predicted, would "probably induce the Enemy to abandon the province of Upper Canada without Opposition."

Madison approved the plan, as well as strikes against Niagara and Montreal. In late May—more than three weeks before the declaration of war—400 regular soldiers and 1,600 militiamen amassed in central Ohio. At the beginning of June they started out on a journey that would take them through vast tracts of forest and swamp, where they would be plagued by wet weather, flies, mosquitoes, and the constant fear of attack from native warriors. For frontiersmen who had been reared on tales of Indian atrocities, Hull's warning that they would be travelling over "ground stained with the blood of your fellow-citizens" was more frightening than inspiring.

Hull made the tortuous eastward journey close to unbearable by his insistence on fortifying the camp every night against possible native attack. On July 1, the Americans reached the Maumee River at the western tip of Lake Erie, where Hull decided to ease the difficulty of transporting his personal belongings somewhat by sending his baggage on northward to Detroit aboard the schooner *Cuyahoga*. Hull was still unaware that Madison had declared war on Great Britain, but the British garrison at Fort Amherstburg had been alerted. *Cuyahoga* sailed down the Maumee, across Lake Erie, then up the Detroit River, accompanied by a second vessel. On July 2, as the two boats approached Amherstburg, the other boat sailed on the west side of Bois Blanc island, but *Cuyahoga* chose the east side, within sight of the British fort. The schooner was captured, along with Hull's possessions. The collection, which included documents and letters that revealed the dissension in his army and his dread of native attack, would prove to be a trump card for Brock.

On July 5, Hull and his army reached Detroit. Although they outnumbered the garrison at Fort Amherstburg, Hull hesitated for a week, then opted for a nearer target, the hamlet of Sandwich. Although Lieutenant-Colonel T. B. St. George, commander at Amherstburg, led men to repel invaders, he placed them too far south and so the Americans crossed into Canada unopposed on July 12. Surprised and frightened, most of the residents of Sandwich fled, allowing Hull to set up his headquarters in the new, not-quite-finished Georgian house owned by prominent businessman and politician François Baby. Hull and Baby had been acquainted before the war, but their friendship did nothing to deter American troops from looting Baby's house. They also destroyed fences and fruit trees, and stole livestock, blankets, and personal items from other residents of the village.

In spite of the looting, Hull stated in a proclamation issued on July 13, "I come to *find* enemies not to *make* them. I come to *protect* not to *injure* you." He urged the residents of the area to stay peacefully at home, promising they would not be harmed if they offered no resistance. "The United States offers you *Peace, Liberty,* and *Security.* Your choice lies between these & *War, Slavery,* and *Destruction.*" He also included a threat designed to keep the militia out of action. *"No white man found fighting by the Side of an Indian will be taken prisoner. Instant destruction will be his Lot."* Hull had copies of the proclamation made, then sent out riders to distribute them throughout the western province. His words, as well as the presence of his army, had the desired effect. Between July 8 and July 15, nearly half of the 850 militia stationed at Fort Amherstburg deserted, while American sympathizers like Andrew Westbrook of Delaware Township encouraged settlers to accept Hull's offer of protection.

On July 22, Brock responded to Hull's proclamation with one of his own, describing the American general's offer of protection as an insult and warning the citizenry that siding with the United States might ultimately make them subjects of Napoleon Bonaparte. He also reassured Upper

Canadians that Britain would not abandon the province. And then he addressed Hull's threat to kill anyone fighting alongside native warriors with a philosophical argument. "By what new principle are they to be prevented from defending their property?...they are men, and have equal rights with other men to defend themselves and their property when invaded, more especially when they find in the enemy's camp a ferocious and mortal foe." To summarily execute whites fighting alongside natives in common cause was not only inconsistent, Brock argued, but tantamount to murder and would be revenged.

On July 16, shortly before the proclamation was issued, the first encounter between American and British troops took place at the Canard River, between Amherstburg and Sandwich. A small group of regulars from the Forty-First, along with some militiamen and native warriors, exchanged fire with Third Ohio Volunteers commanded by Colonel Lewis Cass. Two British soldiers, privates James Hancock and John Dean, were wounded and taken prisoner. Hancock died that evening, becoming the first British fatality of the war.

Unable to fend off the Americans, Lieutenant John Clemow retreated towards Amherstburg, but skirmishing continued over the next few days. Surprisingly, although the invading American army outnumbered the British-Canadian force at Amherstburg two to one, Hull did not press his advantage. Instead, he met repeatedly with his officers to discuss strategy without coming to any firm decision. Aside from fearing his men might be massacred by native warriors if he engaged the British, Hull was also concerned about supplying his forces. Provisions had to be transported 320 km through the wilderness because the land around Detroit lacked the resources to sustain his army.

While Hull hesitated, Brock was wrestling with low morale in Upper Canada. The Six Nations' refusal to commit to the war continued to irk him. He suspected that they were only waiting for an American victory, at which point they would spring into action, cut off transportation and supply routes, and then show "their true disposition" by committing "everything horrid." He was not much more impressed with the white population. "The disaffected became more audacious and the wavering more intimidated," he wrote at one point after the American invasion.

Long before war was declared, Brock and others had had certain reservations about the loyalty of the militia of Upper Canada. Although an estimated eleven thousand men were available for militia service, it was thought safe to arm only four thousand. But even Brock had apparently not anticipated that the militia would actually refuse to obey orders. In July 1812, Colonel Thomas Talbot, who commanded the militia in the London District, was instructed to recruit men to march westward to the Thames River to keep the Americans at bay. As part of the recruitment effort he visited Norfolk

County, where he hoped to round up a hundred local militia-men. When word of his intentions reached the area, justice of the peace John Beemer and others discussed their options. Talbot arrived expecting compliance. Instead, he was met by "a large assembly of farmers with their women, who upon my approach addressed me by declaring that their men should not march." Beemer added his voice to those of the women, stating that he thought it "highly improper" to withdraw the militia from the area. Aware of the Six Nations' refusal to commit to the war effort, the settlers were unwilling to leave their homes undefended. Many miles to the east, the Niagara militia also refused to march for the same reason.

On July 29, Brock described his position as "most critical"—not because of the enemy's occupation of the western province, but because of the attitude prevalent among the "vile population" of Upper Canada. "The popu-lation...is essentially bad," he wrote. Everyone, he claimed, including legislators, magistrates, and militia officers, fully believed that the province would be lost to the Americans, and because of this they made little or no effort to repel them. Adding to Brock's woes were American sympathizers, who, emboldened by Hull's occupying army, were "allowed to parade the country without interruption and commit all imaginable mischief."

But that same day, July 29, Brock received word that Michilimackinac had fallen into British-Canadian hands. It gave him reason to celebrate. But Hull, who had learned of the loss of Fort Mackinac on July 26, was plunged further into despair by the news. He was convinced "Savages from the North" would soon attack his army. Instead, the attack came from the south, where the Wyandot rejoiced at the news of the British-Canadian victory. On August 5, native warriors under Tecumseh ambushed a contingent of two hundred Ohio militia commanded by Major Thomas Van Horne at Brownstown, 40 km south of Detroit. The American party had left Detroit the day before, to rendezvous with soldiers bringing needed supplies and cattle to Hull's army. Although Captain Brush, the commander of the relief column, had requested Hull to send an escort because he was aware of the possibility of an attack by natives and British regulars, Van Horne's men were caught by surprise. Eighteen Americans were killed in the skirmish, twelve were wounded, and seventy disappeared, while only one native warrior was killed.

Not only did the ambush reinforce Hull's fears about native attacks, but it also cut his supply and communications line. This, along with the arrival of reinforcements at Fort Amherstburg, made it difficult for him to continue his occupation of Canadian territory. Starting on the night of August 7 and continuing through the early hours of August 8, he pulled most of his men back across the Detroit River, leaving only a small detachment at Sandwich.

Far to the east, Brock had called an emergency session of the Legislature, hoping to persuade it to implement the measures they had refused to consider earlier in the year. While they did vote money for the militia, they again refused to suspend *habeas corpus*. Brock prorogued Parliament and gave orders for a rendezvous of troops and transport at Dover on Lake Erie on the first leg of a journey to Amherstburg. He sailed from York to the Head-of-the-Lake (now Hamilton). According to tradition, he and his officers spent the night with politician and businessman James Durand before riding cross-country the following morning to the Grand River in one more attempt to persuade the Six Nations to join the war effort. Response was lukewarm, but he was promised that sixty warriors would be sent to Amherstburg.

Brock then headed south towards Lake Erie, stopping just south of present-day Simcoe at a tavern owned by William Culver to rally volunteers in Norfolk County. Less than a month earlier, Thomas Talbot had failed abysmally at the same task. This time, Brock's confidence and charm were irresistible. There was no difficulty getting volunteers, even from among men who had a good reason to be excused from service. According to local tradition, one fellow named Cole stepped forward but was initially dismissed because he was blind in one eye. That wouldn't be a problem, he replied. Most men closed one eye when taking aim, but since he was partly blind "he would be saved the trouble of shutting his eye, and for that reason could shoot more rapidly than the others." Brock was tickled by the man's can-do attitude and allowed Cole to join the expedition.

Brock and his officers spent the night at Robert Nichol's estate in Dover. As soon as war was declared, Brock had appointed his old friend quartermaster-general of militia for Upper Canada. In the few days since the legislature had been prorogued, Nichol and his assistant, James Cummings of Chippawa, had pulled together the vessels and supplies needed for the trip westward.

It turned out to be a miserable journey—wet, windy, and often unseasonably cold. On August 8, the very day that William Hull finished moving his men back across the Detroit River, fifty soldiers of the Forty-First regiment, augmented by 250 men from the Lincoln, Norfolk, Oxford, and York militia companies, set sail from Dover. On August 10, it was so windy that the boats put into Port Talbot rather than risk being swamped by Lake Erie's waves. The following day, Brock decided to keep going after dark, in spite of continuing wet weather. In his orders, he warned his men to keep their weapons and ammunition ready as they were passing through territory "known to have been visited by the enemy's patrols." He also stipulated that the boats were to stay behind his own vessel and be guided by the light in it.

Up to that point, the boats had put ashore when conditions warranted, but on August 12, noting that the coast was "more dangerous and difficult of access," Brock gave orders not to land unless absolutely necessary and to do so with extreme caution. Again, partly to make up for lost time, partly to elude any enemy that might be lurking along the coastline, the small flotilla sailed at night.

Pitching about in small boats in rainy, windy weather, sustained by a monotonous diet of pork and bread, worried whether the next few days might bring death or imprisonment, the men had every right to be downhearted, but Brock's leadership skills made all the difference. At one point, the boat he was on hit a rock and stuck fast. When oars and poles failed to budge her, Brock jumped overboard and was immediately followed by the rest of the men. Relieved of their weight, the boat floated off the rock. As soon as everyone was safely back on board, Brock took out his liquor case and made sure every man received a "Glass of Spirits to prevent injury from their wet clothes." The story of Brock's actions quickly spread among the men, further enhancing his reputation. And Brock was equally impressed by their performance under trying circumstances: "In no instance have I witnessed greater cheerfulness...and it is but justice to this little band to add that their conduct throughout excites my admiration."

After days fighting the waves on Lake Erie, the little flotilla finally turned northwards into the Detroit River. Just before midnight on August 13, they anchored at Amherstburg. On Bois Blanc Island, in the Detroit River opposite the fort,

Tecumseh and his natives greeted the arrival of Brock's flotilla by firing their weapons into the air. Brock appreciated the gesture, but through Matthew Elliott relayed the message that they should save their ammunition.

Brock was already acquainted with Elliott. The elderly trader and Indian Department agent had been born in Ireland, but had spent most of his life in North America. After the American Revolution he had settled south of Amherstburg, establishing a large, fine estate while continuing his involvement in business and politics. Brock, who had visited the Detroit area sometime before September 1810, was aware that Elliott had considerable influence with the native people and thought him "an exceedingly good man." His major fault was that he was too supportive of native concerns, "biased and prejudiced," in Brock's judgment. But there was little possibility of involving the natives in the attack on Detroit without Elliott's participation.

Even more important was Tecumseh's support. Soon after Brock landed, Elliott was sent to ask Tecumseh to come to Brock. One of Brock's aides-de-camp, Captain John Glegg, wrote a description of his arrival. The celebrated native leader was dressed in a fringed buckskin jacket and matching fringed trousers, as well as moccasins decorated with dyed porcupine quills. From his aquiline nose dangled three small silver crowns and around his neck was a silver medallion bearing the image of King George III. He was tall, slender, and well-built, with a "light copper" complexion and hazel eyes "beaming cheerfulness, energy, and decision." The two war leaders greeted each other cordially, sizing each other up, each assessing whether all they had heard about the other was credible. Then, because Brock and his men were tired from their long journey, they parted with promises to speak at length the following day.

Chapter 5
Hero of Upper Canada

In the summer of 1812, Tecumseh was arguably the most influential native man in eastern North America, although only a few years previously he had been overshadowed by his older brother, Tenskwatawa. Born around 1775 and initially called Lalawethika, "noisemaker," Tenskwatawa had a troubled childhood and young manhood, losing the sight of his right eye in an accident, becoming addicted to alcohol, and failing at almost everything he did including marriage, hunting, and fighting. Then, in 1805, he began having visions and emerged as a spiritual leader. Renamed "the Prophet"—Tenskwatawa—he preached a return to traditional native culture. He urged his fellow Shawnee and others to avoid European clothing, weapons, and alcohol and to stop selling their land to the American government.

Although there were many among the Shawnee and other tribes who thought the Prophet's message wrong-headed and dangerous, others took his words to heart. His influence was great enough to attract the interest of the British, who decided he would make a useful ally. An attempt was made to arrange a meeting between the Prophet and Lieutenant-Governor Francis Gore at Amherstburg in the summer of 1808, but because of the hostility of other Shawnee leaders, Tenskwatawa chose to stay away. Instead, he sent Tecumseh, who quickly impressed Gore as "a very shrewd intelligent man."

Tecumseh was forty at the time, eighteen months older than Brock. He had embraced his brother's teaching to a great extent, wearing traditional native dress, and, according to tradition, choosing not to marry the woman he loved, because she was white. But Tecumseh also understood the political power inherent in the Prophet's message, especially if it served to unite the American tribes. That, in fact, was a goal Tecumseh was actively working towards, and in 1809 he began a long journey to various native groups south of the Great Lakes, bringing the message of a pan-Indian confederation.

In September 1809, Indiana Territory governor William Henry Harrison concluded the Treaty of Fort Wayne, which turned over more than a million hectares of native land to the government of the United States. Tecumseh and his

supporters loudly opposed the deal, which involved brib-
ery and great quantities of free liquor. The conflict between
Harrison and white settlers on one side and Tecumseh
and his supporters came to a climax in November 1811
at the Battle of Tippecanoe. Prophetstown, Tenskwatawa's
headquarters, was destroyed and many of his followers dis-
illusioned. But Tecumseh's power remained largely intact,
especially after a December earthquake was interpreted by
many native groups as a sign that he and the Prophet must
be supported. Six months later, the declaration of war offered
Tecumseh and his followers the chance to achieve their goals
through an alliance with the British.

On August 14, having recuperated somewhat from
his journey along Lake Erie, Brock spoke to a gathering
of approximately a thousand natives, telling them that he
planned to drive the Americans from Detroit and asking for their assistance. This plan was exactly what they
wanted to hear. In fact, Tecumseh was so impressed that he
turned to some of his companions and, pointing at Brock,
exclaimed, "Ho! This is a man!" Native support solidified
when Tecumseh spoke in support of Brock's scheme. But the
details were not for general consumption. After addressing
the main group, Brock led his officers to Matthew Elliott's
estate, about 15 km south of Amherstburg, for a more private
meeting. Here, Brock laid out his strategy, which Tecumseh
supported wholeheartedly. Even though the capture of Hull's

"Surrender of Hull," by Henry Louis Stephens

papers had made the Americans' vulnerability clear, only one of Brock's officers approved the plan. Robert Nichol, of whom it was said was so devoted to the general that he would follow him into a volcano, not only agreed, but, having spent a few years as an apprentice in Detroit, also offered to guide Brock to any point in the town he wished to go.

Having allowed his officers to express their misgivings, Brock then asked for their support and received it. Over the next hours, the detailed plans came together. By the following afternoon, five British guns were in place on an elevated spot across from Detroit. For several hours the two sides exchanged fire, then, because no progress was being made, ceased temporarily.

Meanwhile, Brock had divided his men into three small brigades. Fifty members of the Royal Newfoundland Regiment and the militia from Essex and Kent formed one group. The second was made up of another fifty regulars, this time from the Forty-First, along with the men of the Lincoln, Norfolk, Oxford, and York militias. The third was completely comprised of regulars, two hundred men from the Forty-First. In addition, about six hundred native warriors, among them Shawnees, Delawares, Potawatomis, Wyandots, Ojibways, Ottawas, and Iroquois, would be led by Matthew Elliott. As promised, the Six Nations Iroquois of the Grand had sent about sixty men under Captain John Norton, but many of them had changed their minds en route, as was their right.

By the time Norton reached Amherstburg, only about half of them remained.

Before the men were deployed, Brock addressed the troops. While some congratulations were in order because the enemy had pulled back across the river, it was also necessary to talk about the large number of desertions from the militia. Brock chose to allow the men to save face, stating that he believed they had been motivated by a need to tend to their farms. But he also rewarded those who had kept to their posts by announcing that immediate arrangements would be made to distribute any back pay.

That same day, August 15, Brock sent General Hull an ultimatum. Hinting that he was backed by a huge military force, he demanded the immediate surrender of Fort Detroit. "It is far from my inclination to join in a war of extermination; but you must be aware, that the numerous body of Indians who have attached themselves to my troops, will be beyond my control the moment the contest commences." Like Roberts at Michilmackinac, Brock was hoping to use the Americans' fear of native warriors to his advantage. The message was carried to Hull by Brock's aide-de-camp, John Glegg, who was kept waiting two hours for a response that was surprisingly confident, given Hull's erratic behaviour over the previous days. "I have no other reply to make than to inform you, that I am prepared to meet any force which may be at your disposal, and any consequences which may result from any exertion of it you may think proper to make."

During the night of August 15–16, Elliott led his men across the Detroit River some distance south of the American fort. Around three in the morning, the British-Canadian force began their crossing at a spot between the River Rouge and Springwell. It was an obvious place for fording the river and Hull had sent men there with orders to stay put unless it became impossible to hold their position. But before Elliott and the warriors arrived, the Americans withdrew, leaving the area open to invasion. Once within sight of the fort, the native warriors created the illusion of a much larger force by wandering through the trees, allowing themselves to be seen, then backtracking while out of sight before again making themselves visible to the Americans. On his side, Brock also created the illusion of more regular troops by having members of the militia dress in cast-off scarlet army tunics.

By morning, the regulars and militia were also across, along with five pieces of light artillery. Brock rode at the front of the troops as they closed the distance between their landing site and Fort Detroit, giving his friend Robert Nichol cause for concern. Brock's size, his scarlet uniform, and its gleaming gold epaulets made him an easy target, and Nichol said so, suggesting that the troops be allowed to go ahead of the general to lessen his exposure to potentially lethal enemy fire. "If we lose you, we lose all," he warned. Characteristically, Brock refused the sensible suggestion. "Master Nichol, I duly appreciate the advice you give me, but I feel that in addition to their sense of loyalty and duty, many here follow me from a feeling of personal regard, and I will never ask them to go where I do not lead them."

Brock was well aware that the Americans were in an excellent defensive position, so he hoped to draw them out onto open ground in front of the fort. But then, with American forces under McArthur and Cass still some distance away, he decided to launch an attack. The guns at Sandwich had resumed firing, landing cannonballs at first in the town of Detroit, and then finally reaching the fort. Five American soldiers were killed, including two officers, one of whom was the same Porter Hanks who had surrendered Fort Mackinac a few weeks earlier.

American gunners were ready to fire on the advancing British-Canadian troops, but no order was given. Inside the fort, Hull was falling apart due to the combined effects of alcohol, drugs, and his own paranoia. He crouched in corners, trembling, worrying about his wife, his daughter and her family, other civilians, and the soldiers under his command. The fort was crowded, packed with refugees from the town as well as American troops, all braced for another round of fire from the British guns across the river. Finally, without consulting any of his officers, Hull raised a flag of truce—a white tablecloth, large enough to be seen from the Canadian shore—then wrote a note asking for a ceasefire and asked his son to deliver it to Brock, who he believed was still on the Canadian side.

It was around ten o'clock, and Brock and his troops were within a mile of the fort when the white flag was spotted. A short time later, Hull's note was delivered. Once again, Captains Glegg and Macdonnell were sent to the fort. Not long afterwards, Glegg returned to inform Brock that Hull was ready to surrender. At Brock's command, he went back to tell Hull that arrangements must be completed within three hours, and to work out the details.

For the next hour or so, British regulars, Upper Canadian militia, and native warriors watched and waited. Then one of the aides-de-camp returned to report that the mission was accomplished. Hull had not only surrendered Fort Detroit, along with all the troops present and those under McArthur and Cass who were still in the field, but in his capacity as governor he had also given up the entire Michigan territory. It was a stunning turn of events.

Military ceremony, steeped in centuries of tradition, could often be used to lessen the pain and humiliation of defeat. Hull, the old Revolutionary soldier, was noted for his love of display. As he went over the details of the surrender, he asked for the honours of war. The ceremonial procession allowed a defeated army that had fought well to march out fully armed and with all flags flying. But the Americans had not fought at all, except for firing heavy guns at the Canadian shore, and Brock correctly refused the request. After British-Canadian forces formed two lines, one on either side of the fort's gates, the Americans slowly emerged from the fort. They were poorly dressed and many of them were apparently ill, according to eyewitness Charles Askin. After marching by their enemies, they piled their weapons outside the fort, then waited. Shortly after noon, the British entered the fort as a regimental band played "The British Grenadiers." Inside, the Stars and Stripes was lowered and replaced with the British flag, then British soldiers fired a seventeen-gun salute with captured American armaments. Tecumseh and other warriors joined in the volley by firing their weapons.

Without losing a single man, Brock had defeated a far larger force and gained a significant victory. Aside from inflicting a second humiliating defeat on the Americans, the British-Canadians had captured a large array of armaments and ammunition, a number of bateaux and boats, and wagons, horses, furs, food, and money. Some of it would be used as the war continued, but some of it would also be distributed among the victors. Every soldier and militiaman involved received a monetary award, and Brock garnered £214, more than he earned in two months as lieutenant-governor.

Money was not the only reward. Brock was lavish in his praise of the regulars, the militia, and the native warriors, stressing the natives' restraint in victory. "Two fortifications have already been captured from the enemy without a drop of blood being shed by the hands of the Indians; the instant the enemy submitted, his life became sacred."

Brock sent the Ohio militia home on parole then had Hull and the regulars, along with their families, sent to Fort Erie by water. Eventually they were returned to the United States, where Hull was court-martialled, convicted of treason and cowardice, and sentenced to death. President James Madison pardoned him because of his Revolutionary War record.

Leaving enough men behind to keep the captured territory secure, Brock set sail for the east aboard the *Chippawa*. Along the way, he discussed his plans to attack the Americans at Niagara. With a swift offensive, he reasoned, he could consolidate the victories at Michilimackinac and Detroit, and perhaps bring end to the war. Yet, according to Captain Peter Robinson of the First York militia, Brock had some concerns that his own tendency to hasty action might eventually prove disastrous. On the voyage to Niagara, he was said to remark, "If this war lasts, I am afraid that I shall do some foolish thing, for if I know myself, there is no want of courage to my nature—I hope I shall not get into a scrape."

As it turned out, he would not get an immediate chance for action of any kind. Shortly before Brock had left York to journey west, Sir George Prevost had been notified that the orders-in-council, one of the troublesome bits of British legislation that had so irked the Americans, had been revoked. In Washington, the British minister was discussing the possibility of ending the war. Always the diplomat, Prevost contacted General Henry Dearborn and the two of them agreed to a temporary truce until September 4. In the meantime, both hoped that a permanent peace might be reached. Meanwhile, Major-General Roger Sheaffe had also negotiated a ceasefire with Major-General Stephen Van Rensselaer. For the time being, hostilities were at a standstill.

Under the terms of the agreement, both American and British vessels could move freely along the inland waterways. This allowed the Americans to move ships to Sackets Harbor at the eastern end of Lake Ontario, where they were armed in anticipation of further hostilities. In a letter home, Brock expressed his frustration with the situation. While it would be worthwhile if a lasting peace could be negotiated, if war did resume, "nothing could be more unfortunate than this pause." Despite the frustration, there was much to celebrate, although it took Brock a little while to realize just what he had accomplished at Detroit. In a letter home, he wrote, "I have received so many letters from people whose opinion I value, expressive of their admiration of the exploit, that I begin to attach to it more importance than I was at first inclined." Among those letters was one from prominent judge and politician William Dummer Powell, whose sentiments were likely echoed by many in Upper Canada: "There is something so fabulous in the report of a handful of troops, supported by a few raw militia, leaving their strong post to invade an enemy of double numbers in his own fortress, and making them all prisoners without the loss of a man."

As a battle, the encounter with the Americans was far from spectacular. But the victory had huge political and psychological impact, especially among the native people, who had no taste for European-style victories accompanied by inordinately high casualties. Brock had proven that the Americans could be repulsed, which, by extension, meant native land in British North America could be protected. After Detroit, the Six Nations committed to fighting with the British-Canadians. The victory also had significant impact on the general population, from whom the militia were drawn. "The militia have been inspired by the recent success, with confidence," Brock wrote. "The disaffected are silenced." One anonymous observer noted, "A determination now prevails among the people to defend their country."

The surrender of Detroit also helped strengthen the government's influence. After showing that its troops had the power to defeat an invading American army, the government solidified its position by strictly enforcing the requirement that all militiamen take the oath of allegiance and by prosecuting anyone suspected of treasonous activities. Pro-American sympathy, which had been widespread in the first weeks of the war, was stifled in the aftermath of Detroit.

Brock was also pleased to think that the victory would get some notice in England, in which case he would probably receive some kind of reward that could help his family financially. Soon after receiving word of the surrender of Detroit, Sir George Prevost had sent Brock's report to England via one of his own aides-de-camp, along with a letter praising Brock's ability. Early that fall, the documents were presented to the Prince Regent, whose immediate reaction was to give Brock a knighthood. Meanwhile, the residents of Upper Canada expressed their appreciation and gratitude in their own way. When Brock reached Fort George, he was greeted by crowds of people on horseback and in carriages, who insisted on a speech. Brock accommodated them, then got back to the business of improving the defences of Upper Canada, installing guns captured at Detroit onto the Canadian fort.

With the temporary truce still in effect, Brock sent the militia home to look to their farms, but warned them they might be called up again at a moment's notice. Then he sailed for Kingston to inspect conditions there. On his arrival, he was greeted with a nineteen-gun salute from the militia artillery. He inspected the militia, then attended a special ceremony put together by the local populace, in which various dignitaries expressed their appreciation for the victory at Detroit. Brock acknowledged the praise graciously, then complimented the militia for the role they had played.

Before the day was over, Brock received a letter from

Prevost announcing that the ceasefire with the Americans would be terminated the following day, September 4. Without waiting for daylight, Brock got back on board the ship and headed for Fort George. When he arrived on September 6, he learned that the Americans were gathering in huge numbers on the eastern shore of the Niagara River. "I expect an attack almost immediately," Brock wrote.

He would have to wait more than a month.

Chapter 6
The Battle of Queenston Heights

Anticipating where the Americans might attack had occupied Brock and others for some time. Between Fort Erie and Chippawa, above the falls, the waters of the Niagara River were comparatively calm and easy to navigate. Below the falls, at Queenston, the current was swift—though a crossing could be accomplished from the American side in under fifteen minutes. Further downstream, an invading force would have to contend with the guns at Fort George.

Queenston had another disadvantage for an invading force: the banks of the river were steep, which meant invaders would have to climb some distance while defenders shot at them from the higher ground. And yet, as September progressed, there were signs that the Americans were seriously contemplating an attack from Lewiston, just across the

Niagara River from Queenston.

General Stephen Van Rensselaer was in charge of the Americans there. Van Rensselaer came from a prominent New York family and was a Federalist who had no particular enthusiasm for the war. He had no military experience—his appointment had been partly an attempt to bring other Federalists in line with Madison's policies. Other army officers distrusted Van Rensselaer because of his political views and some spread nasty rumors, including one that Van Rensselaer would surrender his forces as soon as they invaded Canada. Some officers refused to meet with Van Rensselaer to discuss strategy, and one, General Alexander Smyth, who established a training camp at Black Rock before the end of the month, was determined that any invasion would happen upstream, between Chippawa and Fort Erie.

At the beginning of September, Van Rensselaer had nearly eight hundred militiamen under his command, but more than one hundred were sick. They had not been paid for some time, many of them lacked shoes or warm clothing, and they were miserable and contentious. To make matters worse, there were shortages of ammunition, tents, and medical supplies.

Matters did not improve much as the month progressed. By mid-September, Van Rensselaer's militia had doubled in number (and some arrived during the ceasefire, confirming Brock's view that the lull in hostilities would prove advantageous for the Americans), but the men had still not been paid. Many decided they'd had enough and simply headed home. Brock was aware of all this turmoil, and his informants reported that military funerals were an almost daily event. Conditions were so bad that some men actually took the desperate measure of heading for Canada, which led to tragedy for one group from the U.S. Sixth Regiment. Six of seven men drowned trying to make it to the Canadian shore. And the low morale extended all the way to the top. Although he made plans for an attack, Van Rensselaer was convinced that Brock would win the day.

If it had been completely up to him, Isaac Brock would have taken advantage of the situation and attacked the Americans while they were still disorganized and discontent. In mid-September, writing to his brother Savery, he confessed he was in an "awkward predicament" and, if he had been left to follow his instincts, he would "sweep everything before me between Fort Niagara and Buffalo." Clearing the Americans out of their positions along the Niagara River between Lakes Ontario and Erie would have been a significant accomplishment, one that would have further undermined their confidence after the defeats at Michilimackinac and Detroit. But, even if he was now regarded as the saviour of Upper Canada, Brock was still a soldier, and a good soldier followed orders. So he watched and waited as the enemy built batteries across from Fort George, weighing the implication of reports that, as soon as their strength reached seven thousand, the Americans would invade.

Adding to Brock's frustration was Prevost's refusal to send reinforcements from Kingston and points east. When Brock asked for a thousand men, the governor general suggested he pull them from the west end of the province, abandoning Detroit and the Michigan territory if necessary. It seemed a strange solution, given the public reaction to the capture of Detroit, but Prevost was only supporting the official British policy of protecting Montreal, Quebec, and Halifax, at the expense of the rest of Canada if need be. Brock did get some reinforcements, members of the Forty-First who had been stationed in Detroit, but he was absolutely adamant about continuing to hold the territory there that he had so recently conquered.

Never one to sit still when work needed to be done, Brock carried out a number of improvements to his fortifications. At Queenston, a redan—a V-shaped temporary fortification—was constructed and an eighteen-pound gun installed to repel any invaders approaching from the river. He also improved one of the bastions at Fort George, renaming it York bastion and installing a twenty-four-pound gun captured at Detroit. In addition, because he appreciated the importance of swift communication in case of attack, a system of beacons was established between Queenston and Lake Erie. Then, as the number of troops on the American side swelled, he ordered that one-third of all regulars and militia at Fort George stay clothed and armed overnight, and that all troops in the fort have their weapons handy at all times and stand on alert between the first crack of dawn and daylight. Brock was determined there would be no surprise attack on the fort.

In addition to the troops and militia, he also had a number of native warriors at his disposal. In the aftermath of Detroit, more than five hundred Six Nations Iroquois, Delaware, Ojibway, and Mississauga men followed John Norton to the Niagara area. Although they did some scouting, they had little patience for inaction. By early October, at least two hundred had returned to their homes.

There was also one of the most unusual groups of soldiers to participate in the War of 1812 on Canadian soil. Soon after the war broke out, Richard Pierpoint had petitioned Brock for permission to form a small troop of black soldiers. There were about a hundred black men in Upper Canada at the time, most of them freed slaves. Some, like Pierpoint, who was sixty-eight when the War of 1812 began, had earned their freedom—and a grant of land—because of their service with the British army during the American Revolutionary War. They had solid reasons for fighting against the Americans. Slavery was being phased out in Canada and Britain had abolished the slave trade, but it was still in effect in the United States. If the Americans won the war, black men like

Pierpoint would lose their hard-won freedom. Initially, Brock turned down Pierpoint's proposal of a corps of black men who would "stand and fight together," but soon he reconsidered. About thirty-eight men joined the Coloured Corps, which was stationed at Fort George. Because of prevailing racial prejudice, the unit was commanded by a white man. Robert Runchey was a tavern keeper who also belonged to the First Lincoln militia, but his character was so unsavoury that the other members of the militia were happy to be rid of him. He did such a poor job leading the Coloured Corps that by October 1812, Lieutenant James Cooper had been put in command.

Tensions on both sides grew as the days passed. By the beginning of October, Stephen Van Rensselaer was so discouraged with the lack of cooperation from other officers and the conditions of his troops that he was certain any invasion into Upper Canada would fail. "Our best troops are raw," he wrote. Worse, they were cold, because adequate clothing had still not been sent, and they wanted to get home to their families. Yet Van Rensselaer was still determined to make the effort to invade the Canadian side of the river, partly to "wipe away part of...our past disgrace," partly to be able to house his troops in the British-Canadian forts over the winter. If the Americans could gain that foothold before the snows came, they would be in an excellent position when the 1813 campaign season began in the spring.

Before Van Rensselaer could launch an attack, the U.S. Navy struck at the Canadian side, capturing two vessels anchored near Fort Erie. One was the government ship, *Detroit*, carrying one of the cannons captured at Detroit. The other was the North West Company brig, *Caledonia*, which was loaded with furs. As Lieutenant Jesse Elliott's men made off with their prizes, guns from Fort Erie fired at them. *Caledonia* made it into Black Rock, on the American side, but the heavy fire forced Elliott's men to run *Detroit* aground on Squaw Island. Brock arrived after nightfall, assessed the situation, and started making plans to get *Detroit* back. Meanwhile, rather than lose their prize, Elliott's men burned it. The capture of the two boats, right under the noses of British-Canadian troops, irked Brock tremendously. In his report he referred to it as an "unfortunate disaster."

The Americans finally decided to attack two days later, on October 11. More troops and boats gathered at Lewiston, but again poor organization and poor communications thwarted Van Rensselaer's plans. The officer who was supposed to pilot the American boats across the river deserted, many of the oars disappeared, and the attack on Canada had to be delayed.

Early on October 12, Brigade-Major Thomas Evans and Thomas Dickson crossed the Niagara to the American side to discuss an exchange of prisoners of war. Although they carried a flag of truce, the sentry on duty would not let them land.

Nor would he send a message to Van Rensselaer, who usually handled these discussions. Instead, another man came down to the shore and said the prisoners had been moved out of the area and would not be exchanged. That seemed a strange turn of events, but Evans and Dickson quickly realized what was going on: the attack was coming soon. Numerous boats were half-concealed along the shoreline, and Evans reported seeing "a horde of half-savage troops from Kentucky, Ohio and Tennessee."

Brock heard Evans's report at Fort George that evening. He immediately put the militia in the vicinity on full alert, then sent out instructions to have the rest of the men along the frontier ready at a moment's notice. He also took time to write to Prevost, telling him that "an attack is not far distant" and that he was attempting to build the militia strength up to two thousand men. But he still had misgivings about their loyalty and willingness to fight. "I...fear that I shall not be able to effect my object with willing, well-disposed characters. Were it not for the numbers of Americans in our ranks, we might defy all their efforts against this part of the province."

Brock could not know the American enemy's strength with certainty, but he was definitely outnumbered. Van Rensselaer could call on about 4,600 men for the invasion. Brock, on the other hand, could put perhaps 2,340 in the field, nearly half of whom were potentially unreliable. Most of the militia had not seen any combat—Detroit barely counted as a battle—and the three hundred native warriors might change their minds at a moment's notice. When he went to bed, probably half-dressed in case he was summoned during the night, his mind was likely full of thoughts of the coming attack and how he would meet the American offensive.

The night of October 12–13 was extremely windy, so much so that the Americans' preparations were nearly inaudible on the Canadian side. Around four in the morning, the boats began heading for Queenston. But most of the troops had little experience with the Niagara River's strong currents. A number of boats were swept downstream, coming ashore past the village in a little cove used by Queenston merchant Robert Hamilton. Some of the invaders were taken prisoner, others wounded or killed.

Meanwhile, Colonel Solomon Van Rensselaer, an experienced soldier who happened to be General Stephen Van Rensselaer's cousin, had made it to the Canadian shoreline with a small group of soldiers from the Thirteenth U.S. Infantry. He and some of the regulars moved cautiously inland to reconnoitre the territory. Left to their own devices, the soldiers left behind amused themselves by chatting—too loudly, as it turned out. Their talk alerted British-Canadian sentries, and, when the Americans began to climb the heights, the defenders started shooting. Van Rensselaer, who was one of those wounded, immediately ordered his men to take shelter under the bank.

Now the British-Canadians stationed in the Queenston area realized that the long-anticipated invasion was underway. They began firing, using a nine-pound gun in a stone guardhouse on the edge of Queenston, the eighteen-pounder at the redan on Queenston Heights, and a twenty-four-pounder at Vrooman's Point, 1.6 km downstream. The bombardment created chaos among the Americans. Some troops partway across the river headed back to the eastern shore, abandoning boats as soon as they landed and heading for cover. Others died on the river and their small boats, bearing cargoes of corpses, floated past Fort George and towards Lake Ontario.

At six o'clock some American boats were still on the river. On the Canadian shore, a number of invaders climbing towards Queenston village were unchallenged because the British-Canadian troops had been sent closer to the water in an attempt to stop the Americans' crossing. Amazingly, the redan had been abandoned, so American Captain John Wool was able to lead his men into it and take control of the high ground, making it far easier for reinforcements to come across the water.

At Fort George, with the high winds blowing, it was likely impossible for Brock to hear any of the gunfire. But it wasn't long before news of the invasion reached him. Still unsure about the Americans' overall plan, he galloped out for Queenston after giving instructions to several officers. John

Norton was also told to follow, with his men.

As he approached Queenston he met George Jarvis, a fifteen-year-old volunteer with the Forty-Ninth Regiment, just heading for Fort George. Young Jarvis informed the general that the Americans had landed at Queenston. Brock pressed on, passing a flank company of the Third York militia under the command of Captain Duncan Cameron. He waved, probably offered some words of encouragement, and continued his dash to the south. A short time later he reached Vrooman's Point. There were soldiers and a twenty-four-pound gun, but no one was firing it. Brock asked why not, and was told that they couldn't reach the Americans. "It can't be helped," Brock shrugged, and galloped on, reaching Queenston just before 7 a.m.

As American invaders continued to arrive from the eastern shore, Brock took in the situation, then dispatched orders to Roger Sheaffe to bring up both the Forty-First and the militia. The general went back to the north end of Queenston and assembled a light company of the Forty-Ninth, including young George Jarvis. The small band proceeded to the base of the heights at the south end of the village, below the redan the Americans had occupied, where they paused. Brock is said to have told them, "Take a breath, boys—you will need it in a few moments." Above them loomed the steep rise of Queenston Heights. While there were some open spaces, there were plenty of thick wooded areas, more than enough to conceal elements of the enemy.

Up to this point, Brock had remained on horseback. There was a brief exchange of gunfire with the Americans on the high ground, and then a pause. Brock dismounted, pulled his sabre from its scabbard, and, swinging it high, raced uphill, his men close behind.

George Jarvis later wrote down what he witnessed that morning. "He led the way up the mountain at double quick time in the very teeth of a sharp fire from the enemy's riflemen." Somewhere on the Heights, an American took careful aim at the large officer in his bright scarlet tunic and fired. "Our gallant General fell on his left side, within a few feet of where I stood." Brock had been struck in the chest, slightly to the right of centre. Jarvis ran up to him. "Are you much hurt, Sir?" he asked. Brock, unable to speak as his lungs filled with blood, "placed his hand on his breast and made no reply, and slowly sunk down."

Later, legends would grow about Brock's death and his final words. One report claimed he said, "Push on, brave York volunteers," but the Yorks were not with him at the time. Another claimed he gave instructions to hide his body, so that his death would not undercut the morale of Upper Canada's defenders. According to Jarvis, men of the Forty-Ninth immediately shouted, "Revenge the General!" And John Beverley Robinson said that, as several of the soldiers gathered around Brock's remains, an American cannonball

"The Death of Brock at Queenston Heights," by C. W. Jefferys

struck one of them, and he fell across the general.

Brock's body was taken to one of the houses in the village, now empty since the women, children, and elderly people had fled inland at the beginning of the fighting. Soon afterward, Brock's aide-de-camp, John Macdonnell, reassembled the men of the Forty-Ninth and led another charge up the hill. He was mortally wounded in the attempt and died the following day.

John Norton was on his way to Queenston from Fort George when someone he met along the way reported that Brock had been killed and that the enemy was heading towards the fort. Not quite believing the news, Norton took his warriors off the road, seeking cover. He had set off from Fort George with about a hundred and sixty Six Nations men, but en route a number of them became worried about the safety of their own families. Silently they slipped away, so that by the time Norton reached Queenston, along with William Kerr and Joseph Brant's son John, only eighty native fighters remained. They melted into whatever trees or bushes they could find, keeping low to the ground to make it as difficult as possible for the enemy to hit them, showing themselves only long enough to tantalize the Americans or frighten them with bloodcurdling war cries. They were effective enough to keep the Americans from concentrating on the regular troops, but for a time it seemed the invaders would win the day. At one point, during a lull, a number of Americans looted Queenston's houses, including the home of James and Laura Secord. (James was somewhere nearby, fighting in the Lincoln militia and receiving two wounds by the end of the day. Laura had fled with their children to nearby St. David's.)

Roger Sheaffe arrived shortly after 10 a.m. with about seven hundred men. Helped by the efforts of Norton's warriors, he was able to circle around the Americans and force them to retreat. Again, it seemed a surprising victory. Given their superior numbers and the element of surprise on their side, the Americans might have been able to maintain their foothold on the Canadian side of the river. But lackluster leadership and poor discipline turned the tide. On the American shore, the New York militia had waited so long, listening to the sound of gunfire and native war whoops, watching their fellow countrymen die, that they came to the conclusion they were within their rights to refuse to fight on foreign soil. They would not cross to reinforce the troops already at Queenston.

By the end of the day, American casualties included approximately five hundred killed and wounded. About nine hundred were taken prisoner. The British-Canadian losses were sixty killed and another sixty or so wounded, and five Iroquois killed. The win should have been a great cause for celebration. It was the first real battle with the enemy, and the British-Canadians had proved they were up to the task. But the loss of Brock made the victory bittersweet, throwing a shadow of sorrow over what should have been a triumphant occasion.

Sheaffe conscientiously reported to Prevost, conveying, along with news of the American defeat, the loss of his old comrade-in-arms. Brock was, in his estimate, "one of the most gallant and zealous officers in his Majesty's Service, whose loss cannot be too much deplored." While the new commander and leader of the Upper Canadian government wrestled with the responsibilities that Brock's death had suddenly thrust upon him, arrangements were made for a suitable funeral for the fallen hero.

Sheaffe and General Stephen Van Rensselaer initially agreed to a three-day ceasefire, enough time to deal with the wounded and the exchange of prisoners. This was later extended until 4 p.m. on October 19, to allow for Brock's funeral. Van Rensselaer willingly supported this extension, adding that he would arrange for a salute in tribute to Brock's gallantry.

The funeral began at 10 a.m. on Friday, October 16, and, according to one eyewitness, "was the grandest and most solemn I ever witnessed, or that has been seen in Upper Canada." The bodies of both Brock and his aide-de-camp, John Macdonnell, which had lain in state at Government House in Newark, were placed on separate caissons. The road between Government House and Fort George was lined by regulars, militia, and native warriors. Under orders from Roger Sheaffe, the regulars had tied black crepe to their swords and donned black crepe arm bands, which they would wear for a month.

As muffled drums beat and two nineteen-pound guns fired every minute, the funeral cortege slowly made its way to the fort. Macdonnell's was first, followed by Brock's, with nine pallbearers in attendance. Brock's horse was part of the procession, led by four grooms. So were his servants and friends, official mourners, and members of the public.

At Fort George, the coffins were taken to the York bastion, reconstruction of which Brock had recently supervised, and placed side by side. Reverend Robert Addison officiated at the ceremony, which ended with a twenty-one-gun salute. Then the coffins were interred. At sunset, in keeping with Stephen Van Rensselaer's promise, gun salutes were fired from both Fort Niagara, which was opposite Fort George on the American side, and Lewiston.

A few weeks later, a delegation of native leaders, including Six Nations, Huron, Chippawa, and Pottawatomi, travelled to Fort George to pay tribute to the fallen leader. One of them, a chief named Kodeaneyonte, presented eight strings of white wampum to Major General Roger Sheaffe, to wipe away the tears of mourning caused by Brock's loss. A larger belt of wampum was also presented to Sheaffe, to symbolically protect Brock's grave.

Chapter 7
Brock's Legacy

As Brock had predicted, the September ceasefire had dire consequences for the war effort. Before the lakes froze for the winter, the American fleet managed to blockade Kingston harbour, which meant the Americans controlled virtually all traffic on Lake Ontario. It was an omen of things to come. The following year, Americans successfully invaded the Niagara Peninsula and held it for several months. In September, after the British were defeated on Lake Erie, the entire southwestern part of Upper Canada was abandoned by regulars and became the scene of numerous American raids. Civilians, who had largely escaped unscathed during the early months of the war, were increasingly targeted. In December 1813, the town of Newark was burned to the ground before the Americans withdrew across the Niagara

River for the winter. British-Canadians retaliated by burning villages on the American side of the river, leading to further retaliation by Americans in 1814.

Brock's successor, Major-General Roger Hale Sheaffe, was doubly handicapped by his own difficult personality and by Brock's already mythical reputation. When York [Toronto], the capital of Upper Canada, was strongly attacked by Americans in April 1813, he ordered the battery and marine stores destroyed, as well as a half-built ship, then pulled out the troops to preserve them. The decision was extremely unpopular with York's leading citizens, notably the Reverend John Strachan, especially when Americans proceeded to loot and damage private property during their week-long occupation. Sheaffe's decision, though strategically sound, was so widely criticized that it would result in his removal as both commander of the forces in Upper Canada and administrator of the province within a couple of months. Francis de Rottenburg, a Polish-born aristocrat, succeeded him. Although de Rottenburg, who had written a military training manual, was a more than competent officer, he seems to have had little respect for colonials. Robert Nichol, Brock's devoted friend and quartermaster general of militia, was frustrated at de Rottenburg's dismissal of his suggestions for a plan of attack that, he claimed, might have shortened the war considerably. By December, de Rottenburg had been replaced by Gordon Drummond.

Another of Brock's old comrades-in-arms fared better than either Sheaffe or Nichol. Following the Battle of Stoney Creek, in June 1813, James FitzGibbon, by now a lieutenant, asked for permission to form a special group of soldiers to harass the American occupiers in the Niagara region. Permission was granted, and the fifty men who formed FitzGibbon's Green Tigers created such a disturbance that before the month was out, Lieutenant-Colonel Charles G. Boerstler was sent with five hundred troops to put an end to their activities. Before Boerstler could attack, Laura Secord somehow heard of his plans. Determined to warn FitzGibbon, she took a roundabout thirty-two-kilometre walk to his headquarters to deliver her message. While FitzGibbon almost certainly had some inkling of the attack through reports from his own or native scouts, Laura's walk eventually made her the most famous woman of the War of 1812.

On the morning of June 24, as they headed for FitzGibbon's headquarters, Boerstler and his men were attacked by about four hundred native warriors hidden in a stand of beech trees. After about three hours of fighting, the Americans were exhausted and attempted to surrender, but the native forces kept on fighting. Soon afterward, FitzGibbon arrived during a lull in the battle, and, using the same ploy that had worked at Michilimackinac and Detroit, explained to the Americans that he might not be able to prevent the natives' concluding a massacre if the fighting continued. Boerstler surrendered and FitzGibbon received credit for the victory, even though he admitted he had arrived at the very last minute and all the fighting had been done by native warriors.

In April 1814, after Napoleon's abdication, British troops were freed for action in North America and attacked numerous strategic targets effectively, including Washington, D.C. Meanwhile, peace negotiations were taking place in Europe, which led to the signing of the Treaty of Ghent on Christmas Eve of 1814. There was no discussion of a native homeland, or of a buffer zone between British-Canadian and American territory. Instead, the treaty stated that any territory captured during the war would be returned to whoever had held it prior to June 18, 1812. Thousands had died in battle, of injury, or of disease, had seen their homes and crops destroyed, but, in the end, nothing changed significantly. There was not even a clear-cut understanding of who was the victor, who the vanquished—a situation that has continued to this day.

This vagueness is partly because of events early in 1815. Although the Treaty of Ghent was signed on December 24, 1814, it would not take effect until it was ratified by both sides. It took until February for the details to reach Washington, and in the meantime, on January 8, 1815, the British suffered a humiliating defeat at the Battle of New Orleans. That sequence of events—the British defeat at New Orleans, followed by the proclamation of peace a few weeks later—convinced many Americans that they had won the war.

The debate still continues, with Canadians emphasizing that the Americans, who declared war in the first place, did not accomplish what they had set out to do. Canada was not conquered, no Canadian territory stayed for long in American hands, and the British presence in Canada continued strong. And some, on both sides, argue that neither Canadians nor Americans won, but the native people definitely lost. Tecumseh's dream of a pan-Indian confederation vanished with his death at the Battle of the Thames in October 1813. After the Battle of Beaver Dams, native people would never again fight as an independent body on Canadian soil.

In the end, though, the war did serve one purpose. It created a powerful myth for at least part of English Canada, and in doing so laid the foundation for a unique Canadian identity. None of that might have happened without the vision, charisma, and leadership ability of Isaac Brock, who remains the best known and most celebrated figure of the War of 1812.

Brock's legend may well have started to grow during his lifetime, a product of his importance and unusual physical stature. But it certainly gained momentum from the moment of his death. Coming so soon after his victory at Detroit, Brock's death inspired an outpouring of public grief, along with a resolve to do something to commemorate his sacrifice.

Portrait of Major-General Sir Isaac Brock, by George Theodore Berthon

On July 20, 1813, the British Parliament authorized the construction of a memorial in his honour. Created by Richard Westmacott, a marble bas-relief in St. Paul's Cathedral,

London, shows Brock's body cradled by a British soldier while a native warrior looks on.

Although Upper Canada was primarily occupied with the business of defence, in March 1814 legislators found time to approve a motion to build a suitable monument to Brock's "great and brilliant service." Introduced by his old friend Robert Nichol, the suggestion was approved with "unspeakable pleasure" by Gordon Drummond. Initially, the government provided £500 for the monument, a significant sum during wartime. In 1815, another £1,000 was approved, and, in 1826, a further £600.

Getting down to the actual business of building the monument took some time. Eventually, three commissioners were appointed: Nichol, Thomas Clark, and Thomas Dickson. All three were veterans of the War of 1812 and had known Brock personally. In 1823, a call for tenders was issued in the newspapers of Upper Canada. Plans called for a circular stone tower 15 metres high and 5 metres in diameter at the base, to be built on Queenston Heights. Underneath the column would be a vault, wherein Brock's and Macdonnell's bodies would be placed. There would also be a square room at the base of the column to serve as a lobby for visitors, and a spiral staircase leading to an observation deck at the top. Initial plans had called for a statue of Brock to top the column, but this idea was abandoned because of the cost.

By the time the cornerstone was laid, on June 1, 1824,

Robert Nichol was dead, killed when he and his horse and wagon mysteriously plunged into the Niagara gorge on a dark night at the beginning of May. On October 13, the twelfth anniversary of Brock's death, the monument was formally dedicated with the transfer of Brock's and Macdonnell's bodies. Disinterred from their resting places at Fort George, they were transported in a black-draped hearse drawn by four black horses. The road to Queenston was lined with members of the Lincoln militia and curious onlookers. Behind the caskets were chiefs from the Six Nations and a host of other dignitaries. In all, it was estimated that perhaps 1,500 people followed the hearse in a procession which took three hours to travel from Fort George to Queenston. At the monument, thousands more had gathered to witness the solemn ceremony in which Brock and his aide-de-camp were placed in the vault and their coffins covered with stone slabs.

Construction proceeded on the monument, which would be the tallest memorial in North America at the time. Brock's monument would be an important tourist attraction, with the observation deck offering a panoramic view of the Niagara Peninsula. But the presence of tourists also meant someone had to be onsite to take their admission fees and to serve them drinks in the lobby. Lieutenant-Governor Sir Peregrine Maitland suggested that Laura Secord might be a good choice. The Secords, whom he knew personally, were struggling financially, but Laura at first refused the offer.

Then she changed her mind and decided she did want the position, but Thomas Clark, the only surviving commissioner (Dickson had died in January 1825), thought that Robert Nichol's widow was a more deserving candidate. Maitland insisted, but Laura did not get the job. A new lieutenant-governor, Sir John Colborne, unaware of Maitland's pledge, appointed Theresa Nichol in 1831. Soon afterward, Laura Secord expressed her disappointment in a letter to Colborne's secretary.

Brock's monument dominated the landscape around Queenston until Good Friday, April 17, 1840, when someone tried to blow it up. The top was ripped off, the stairs demolished, and the main structure badly cracked. Suspicion fell on Benjamin Lett, a Fenian sympathizer, although it was never proven that he was responsible. Assessing the damage, Francis Hall, the engineer who had built the monument, thought it was possible to repair it but his opinion was not popular. Instead, it was decided to build a new monument. The first design accepted called for a structure without stairs or a lookout, but, after a long delay, this plan was rejected and a new competition for designs opened. William Thomas of Toronto submitted the winning application—a 56-metre tower, topped by a 10-metre statue of Brock with one hand on his sword and his right arm pointing northward. In 1853, the bodies of Brock and Macdonnell were temporarily moved to the Hamilton family cemetery at Queenston, then reinterred

The monument at Queenston Heights viewed from the American shore, c. 1888

at the base of the new monument that October.

Completed in 1857 and located 183 meters west of the original, Brock's new monument was the second-highest memorial of its kind in the world, an impressive tribute to a man who had already become legendary. But it was only one of many tributes to Brock's memory. Aside from the sculpture in St. Paul's Cathedral, there would eventually be a plaque on the house where Brock was born and another on the wall of St. Peter Port Church in Guernsey. One monument at Queenston would indicate the approximate spot where Brock was killed (although the exact location is uncertain). Another monument was erected in memory of Alfred, the horse that

Sir James Craig had offered to send Brock in 1811, although there is no proof that Brock ever accepted him or that Alfred was present at Queenston Heights. Most recently, a bust of Brock was included as part of the Valiants Memorial, dedicated in Ottawa in November 2006. Nineteenth-century poems and songs paid tribute to Brock, his name has appeared on numerous schools and streets, and in 1812 Elizabethtown, Ontario, changed its name to Brockville in his honour.

Brock is also enshrined in many museums, where something of his presence in exhibits about the War of 1812 is mandatory. Occasionally, there is a rare artifact connected directly to him. Some of Brock's personal items eventually found their way back to Canada. The sword and coatee—a short coat—that Brock wore at Queenston were both returned to Guernsey, along with a woven sash (or *ceinture fléchée*) and cravat. The family held these mementos for many years until Brock's grandnieces, Henrietta and Emilia Tupper, decided it would be more appropriate to place them in Canadian institutions. The plain coatee, sash, and cravat went to the Dominion Archives, forerunner of the National Archives and Library of Canada, while another garment, a more formal dress coatee, was donated to the McCord Museum in Montreal. The cravat has since disappeared, but the bullet-holed coatee Brock was wearing at the time of his death is now in the National War Museum. Another piece of clothing, the cocked hat Brock's brother Irving had such trouble about sending in the summer of 1810, eventually did reach Canada, although Brock never wore it. It is now in the Niagara Historical Society Museum in Niagara-on-the-Lake.

In the two centuries since his death, so many stories have been told about Brock that it is often impossible to distinguish myth from reality. According to one tradition, after the capture of Detroit he presented Tecumseh with his red silk officer's sash. In exchange, Tecumseh gave Brock his own woven sash. Although Tecumseh was apparently quite pleased with the gift from Brock, he appeared without it the next day, explaining he had given it to Roundhead, an older chief, as it would have been unseemly for him to wear it in the presence of such a seasoned warrior. As for the woven sash, or *ceinture fléchée*, which Tecumseh gave Brock, and which some chroniclers claim he wore for the rest of his life, that story may be entirely apocryphal. Brock did have such a sash in his possession, but he may have obtained it at any time during his sojourn in the Canadas.

Another story claims that, somewhere between Fort George and Queenston on the last morning of his life, Brock stopped to take a cup of coffee from Sophia Shaw, a young woman whom he planned to marry. Although the two were certainly acquainted, none of his family, friends, or fellow officers had any inkling of an understanding between Brock and Sophia, suggesting that the story evolved so that the Shaw family could bask in the reflected glory of a fallen hero.

Most of the legends portray Brock as larger than life, brave, charming, competent, and generous, and he has few detractors. But there are those who wonder what might have happened if Brock had not conveniently died at the height of his popularity. As the war progressed and the Americans' military competence increased, would his bold impatience have led to a rash decision and a disastrous defeat in which too many lives were lost? Given his minimal combat experience and his devotion to his men, how would he have reacted to a defeat? More importantly, how would the population have reacted? Would the "Saviour of Upper Canada" have fallen from the heady heights he reached after Detroit? Did he ever deserve the title in the first place?

History is full of what-ifs, which make for interesting debates but do nothing to change the past. Whatever legends and half-truths surround Brock and his accomplishments in Upper Canada, the truth is that he was an exceptional man in an exceptional time who accomplished something probably no other individual could have.

Brock's extensive and conscientious preparations for the defence of the Canadas might have been managed by any competent and skilled soldier or administrator. Those preparations went a long way towards preserving the country, Upper Canada in particular. But Brock did something much more significant.

When freed slave Richard Pierpoint first asked

permission to form a black militia unit, he envisioned a group that would "stand and fight together," united in a common cause that not only included the need to defend the land they called home, but also the bitter memory of their shared experience as former slaves. With the exception, perhaps, of those who had fought on the British side during the American Revolutionary War, white settlers in Upper Canada had nothing in particular to unite them except an interest in defending their own properties. The early reluctance of the militia to turn out to fight invaders suggests that most had little concept of a greater good, of anything bigger than their own particular interests. Through the sheer force of his personality, Brock opened their eyes to that greater good, somehow molding recently and not-so-recently arrived American settlers, sons of Loyalists, British regulars, and native warriors into a force that could stand and fight together and defeat a common enemy. Brock's single Canadian victory at Detroit was an unusual, unspectacular, virtually bloodless clash, but it was a turning point that led directly to the formation of a distinct Canadian identity. Ultimately, that is Brock's greatest legacy.

Further Reading

Benn, Carl. *The Iroquois in the War of 1812*. Toronto: University of Toronto Press, 1999. An excellent view of native participation in the war.

Berton, Pierre. *Flames Across the Border*. Toronto, McClelland & Stewart, 1981.

———. *The Invasion of Canada*. Toronto: McClelland & Stewart, 1980. Berton's two books are an entertaining and highly accessible introduction to the War of 1812.

Cruikshank, Ernest A., ed. *The Documentary History of the Campaigns on the Niagara Frontier, 1812–14*. 9 volumes. Welland and Lundy's Lane: Lundy's Lane Historical Society, 1902–8. (Online version at www.ourroots.ca.) An amazing collection of letters and other documents provides a behind-the-scenes look at events in the 1812–1814 era.

FitzGibbon, Mary Agnes. *A Veteran of 1812: The Life of James FitzGibbon*. Toronto, 1894. James FitzGibbon's niece draws on some of her uncle's memories in this book. As one of Brock's protegés, James FitzGibbon was able to provide a number of personal anecdotes about his famous commander. Available online at www.canadiana.org.

Further Reading

Gordon, Irene Ternier. *Tecumseh: Diplomat and Warrior in the War of 1812*. Toronto: Lorimer, 2009. A nicely written introduction to Tecumseh's role in the War of 1812.

Hickey, Donald R. *Don't Give Up the Ship: Myths of the War of 1812*. Urbana and Chicago: University of Illinois Press, 2006. Underpinned by scholarly research, Hickey's book is entertaining, informative, and helps separate fact from legend.

Riley, Jonathon. *A Matter of Honour: The Life, Campaigns and Generalship of Isaac Brock*. Montreal: Robin Brass Studio, 2011. Riley fills in a number of gaps in the story of Brock and, as a career soldier, offers compelling insights into the challenges he faced and into his actions.

Turner, Wesley B. *The Astonishing General: The Life and Legacy of Sir Isaac Brock*. Toronto: Dundurn Press, 2011. Solidly researched, although Brock's story often disappears amid Turner's vast knowledge of the period. The book has some very interesting appendices, including a timeline, Brock's speeches, and an inventory of Brock's effects at the time of his death.

Acknowledgements

The author wishes to acknowledge the assistance provided by Library and Archives Canada; War of 1812 re-enactors Dave Westhouse, Roy Winders, and Zig Misiak for their prompt assistance in directing me to valuable sources of information; John MacLeod of Fort Malden for some important insight into Brock's movements in the Amherstburg area; Amy Klassen, Niagara Historical Society & Museum, for information on the whereabouts of some of Brock's effects; my husband Dan Riley for his patience while I visited and photographed every site related to Brock and the War of 1812 in the Windsor/Amherstburg area; and my very good friend Bob Blakeley for inspiring my interest in the War of 1812 and for the hours of discussion on that topic. And last, but definitely not least, many thanks to proofreader Jacqui Hartley and copy editor Laurie Miller, whose work considerably improved the manuscript.

About the Author

Cheryl MacDonald has been writing about Canadian history for nearly thirty years. She is a full-time writer and historian whose weekly history column has appeared in the *Simcoe Times-Reformer* and its forerunner for a quarter century, and whose historical articles have been published in *The Beaver*, *Maclean's*, the *Hamilton Spectator*, and *The Old Farmer's Almanac*.

Cheryl has written, co-authored, or edited forty books on Canadian and Ontario history, among them *Norfolk, Haldimand and the War of 1812, including the Six Nations* (with Bob Blakeley), and various Amazing Stories titles, such as *Laura Secord*, *Lethal Ladies*, and *Shipwrecks of the Great Lakes*. Cheryl has a master's degree in history from McMaster University, and when not writing or researching can usually be found presenting talks on historical topics. You can reach Cheryl through her website, www.heronwoodent.ca.

Photo Credits

Index